Madley Church from the east.

THE OLD PARISH CHURCHES OF HEREFORDSHIRE

CONTENTS

GLOSSARY OF ARCHITECTURAL TERMS

Abacus	- A flat slab on top of a capital.
Apse	- Semi-circular or polygonal east end of a church containing an altar.
Ashlar	- Masonry of blocks with even faces and square edges.
Baldacchino	- A canopy supported on columns.
Ballflower	- Globular flower of three petals enclosing a ball. Current c1310-40.
Baroque	- A whimsical and odd form of the Classical architectural style.
Beakhead	- Decorative motif of bird or beast heads, often biting a roll-moulding.
Broaches	- Sloping half pyramids adapting an octagonal spire to a square tower.
Chancel	- The eastern part of a church used by the clergy.
Chevron Ornament	- A Norman ornament with a continuous series of Vs forming a zig-zag.
Clerestory	- An upper storey of part of a church, pierced by windows.
Collar-Beam	- A tie-beam used higher up nearer the apex of a roof.
Corbel Table	- A row of corbels supporting the eaves of a roof.
Crossing Tower	- A tower built on four arches in the middle of a cruciform church.
Cruciform Church	- A cross-shaped church with transepts forming the arms of the cross.
Cusp	- A projecting point between the foils in a foiled Gothic arch.
Dado	- The decorative covering of the lower part of a wall or screen.
Decorated	- A division of English Gothic architecture roughly from 1290 to 1360.
Dog Tooth	- Four cornered stars placed diagonally and raised pyramidally.
Early English	- The first division of English Gothic architecture from 1200 to 1290.
Easter Sepulchre	- A recess in a chancel which received an effigy of Christ at Easter.
Elizabethan	- Of the time of Queen Elizabeth I (1558-1603).
Fan Vault	- A vault with blank fan-like tracery emanating from pendants.
Foil	- A lobe formed by the cusping of a circle or arch.
Four Centered Arch	- A flat arch with each curve drawn from two compass points.
Hammerbeam Roof	- A roof carried on arched braces set on beams projecting from a wall.
Herringbone Masonry	- Courses of stones alternately sloping at 45 degrees to horizontal.
Hoodmould	- A projecting moulding above an arch or lintel to throw off water.
Indent	- A shape chiselled out of a stone to receive a memorial brass, etc.
Jacobean	- Of the time of King James I (1603-25).
Jamb	- The side of a doorway, window, or other opening.
King-Post	- An upright timber connecting a tie-beam with a collar-beam.
Lancet	- A long, comparatively narrow window, usually with a pointed head.
Light	- A compartment of a window.
Lintel	- A horizontal stone or beam spanning an opening.
Miserichord	- Bracket underneath hinged choir stall seat to support standing person.
Mullion	- A vertical member dividing the lights of a window.
Nave	- The part of a church in which the congregation is accommodated.
Nook Shafts	- Shafts set in the angle of a pier, respond, or jamb of an opening.
Norman	- A division of English Romanesque architecture from 1066 to c1200.
Ogival Arch	- Arch of oriental origin with both convex and concave curves.
Perpendicular	- A division of English Gothic Architecture from c1360 to c1540.
Pilaster	- Flat buttress or pier attached to a wall. Common in Norman period.
Piscina	- A stone basin used for rinsing out holy vessels after a mass.
Plinth	- The projecting base of a wall.
Queen-Posts	- Two vertical timbers connecting a tie-beam and a collar-beam.
Quoins	- The dressed stones at the corners of a building.
Rere-Arch	- An arch on the inside face of a window enbrasure or doorway.
Reredos	- A structure behind an altar. Usually sculpted or painted.
Respond	- A half-pier or column bonded into a wall, and carrying an arch.
Reticulation	- Tracery with a net-like appearence. Fashionable in c1330-60.
Rood Screen	- A screen with a crucifix mounted on it between a nave and chancel.
Saxon	- Division of the English Romanesque style from the 6th century to 1066.
Sedilia	- Seats for priests (usually three) on the south side of a chancel.
Tester	- A sounding board above a 17th century pulpit.
Tie-Beam	- A beam connecting the slopes of a roof at or near its foot.
Tracery	- The intersecting ribwork in the upper part of a later Gothic window.
Transom	- A horizontal member dividing the lights of a window.
Triptych	- Three surfaces, usually sculpted or painted, joined by hinges.
Tympanum	- The space between the lintel of a doorway and the arch above it.
Victorian	- Of the time of Queen Victoria (1837-1901).
Wall Plate	- A timber laid longitudinally along the top of a wall.
Wind-Braces	- The struts used to strengthen the sloping sides of a gabled roof.

ARCHITECTURAL INTRODUCTION

THE SAXON PERIOD

The district which from the early 11th century until 1974 formed the county of Herefordshire was converted to Christianity in the 7th century. It is likely that the county contained about fifty churches at the time of the Norman Conquest and certainly all those with dedications to obscure Celtic saints are early foundations. Some of these buildings may only have been of wood, and those that were constructed of stone have been so rebuilt over the centuries as to leave no remains. The NE corner of the nave at Kilpeck, with a typically Saxon arrangement of alternate long and short quoins, may be the only standing masonry of the period in the county. There are in addition loose or re-set carved stones at Llanveynoe, Munsley, Cradley, and Acton Beauchamp. The latter is the most important.

THE EARLY NORMAN PERIOD

The boom in the construction of new stone parish churches did not begin until two generations had passed since the Norman Conquest. Work which is likely to be of the period 1066-1130 appears only in about ten parish churches. Herringbone masonry with stone courses alternately sloping at 45 degrees to vertical appears in the naves at Wigmore, Letton, Munsley, Hatfield, and Edvin Loach, whilst the nave at Bredwardine has early looking doorways. These naves all had the principal entrance on the south side, but sometimes there was a second doorway opposite in the north wall. Small round headed windows with glass or shutters flush with the outside wall-face, and wide internal splays, gave only minimal light. In the east wall would be a round arch opening onto a small chamber called a chancel which contained the altar. Some chancels were square ended from the start, but others were originally apsed until altered later, as at Bredwardine. The much more spacious chancels to accommodate choirs were a later development as far as ordinary parish churches are concerned. Only the much larger churches of Hereford Cathedral and Leominster Priory possessed side aisles in this period with large round piers supporting plain round arches.

THE 12th CENTURY

Half of the churches described in the gazetteer have a 12th century nave or chancel, or both, still standing, even if usually in a much altered state. Others have fonts, re-set doorways and windows, or other loose fragments of the period. Virtually all the churches in this book had been established by the year 1200. Herefordshire has remained a pastoral county with little population growth in many of the villages, and this helps to explain the high proportion of Norman work still remaining in the parish churches. Many English parish churches were enlarged in the later medieval period by the addition of aisles, but two thirds of the churches described in this book still have unaisled naves, and only a ninth have aisles on both north and south sides of the nave. So, although the later centuries often provided larger new windows, new roofs, a wealth of furnishings and memorials, and replaced crumbling sandstone and limestone walling as necessary, expansion of the seating area for the congregation was not often embarked upon.

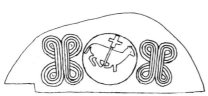

Tympanum at Byton Church

Tympanum in Fownhope Church

Parish churches of the period 1135-80 follow the same general pattern as before. Kilpeck and Moccas are almost unaltered examples of three-celled churches, with a square chancel set between a nave and an apse. Peterchurch has four cells, the extra compartment set between the nave and chancel being the base of a former tower. No other churches have surviving apses but traces of them have been found at Tarrington and Mathon. Fownhope has a central tower still in a fairly complete state, and transepts survive from cruciform churches with central towers at Bromyard and Madley.

Herefordshire is particularly noted for architectural sculpture in this period, and especially the work of a master craftsman and his followers who are referred to as The Herefordshire School. The earliest work by the master appears at Shobdon in c1135-45. In the 1140s he was at work on the south doorway at Kilpeck, and in c1150 he or close associates produced the tympana at Brinsop, Leominster, Stretton Sugwas, Fownhope, and St Giles Hospital at Hereford. The chancel arch at Kilpeck is also by a member of the workshop, but not the master, whilst the fonts at Castle Frome and Eardisley may be slightly later. These examples show sculpture of great intensity with long narrow figures and beasts with long claws, and was inspired by Anglo-Saxon and Viking sculpture plus contemporary work in North Italy, Western France, and at Reading Abbey, the mother house of Leominster Priory. So perhaps the workshop originated in craftsmen assembled in c1125 to work on the lost parts of the priory church.

Yatton Chapel: south doorway

Ledbury Church: west doorway

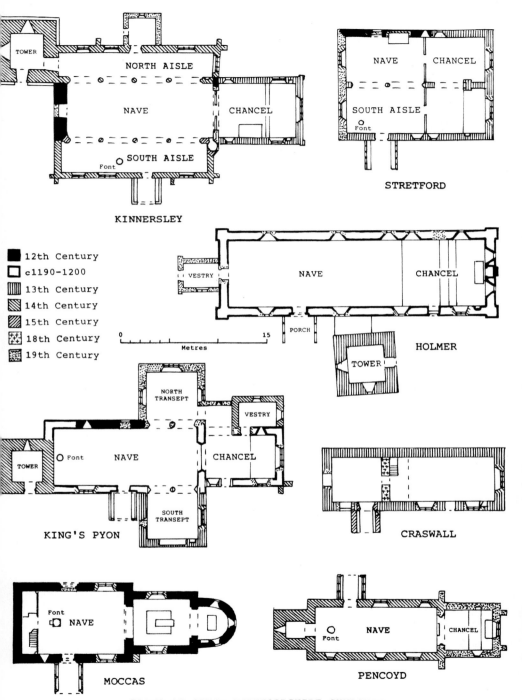

TOWER

NORTH AISLE

NAVE

CHANCEL

Font ○ SOUTH AISLE

KINNERSLEY

NAVE   CHANCEL

SOUTH AISLE

○ Font

STRETFORD

■ 12th Century
□ c1190-1200
▨ 13th Century
▧ 14th Century
▨ 15th Century
▦ 18th Century
▨ 19th Century

VESTRY

NAVE

CHANCEL

PORCH

TOWER

HOLMER

0   15

Metres

NORTH
TRANSEPT

VESTRY

TOWER ○ Font   NAVE   CHANCEL

SOUTH
TRANSEPT

KING'S PYON

CRASWALL

Font
ᑕ▯   NAVE

MOCCAS

NAVE   CHANCEL
○
Font

PENCOYD

PLANS OF SEVEN HEREFORDSHIRE CHURCHES

5

Priest's Doorway
at Canon Pyon

Bromyard Church:
arch of south doorway

During the 1170s and 1180s the Norman style becomes less plain
and massive, and then from the 1190s into the early years of the
13th century gradually gives way to the early Gothic style using
the pointed arch, which in this country is called Early English.
Piers slowly become slenderer, windows are made bigger and there is
a proliferation of motifs such as the zig-zag or chevron ornament
first introduced rather sparingly, and then only in the vertical
plane, in the 1120s. Ledbury has a very long chancel of c1175-85
with typical clasping buttresses at the east corners and two bays
of arches for side chapels, plus a fine nave west doorway of c1200.
Bosbury church has been little altered since it was rebuilt with a
fully aisled nave in the 1190s, and Holmer has one large chamber
serving as nave and chancel, which was quite a common pattern. In
c1180-1200 towers were added at Almeley, Cradley, Dilwyn, Bridge
Sollers, Hampton bishop, Wellington, and Westhide, and aisles were
added at a dozen churches. The arcades are more likely to survive
than the aisle outer walls, as at Weston-Under-Penyard, Bromyard,
and Upton Bishop. At Garway the Templars built a round nave in the
1190s of which the foundations and chancel arch still survive.

THE 13th CENTURY

Apart from the insertion of new doorways and windows in older walls,
a third of Herefordshire's medieval churches have structural work
of the 13th century. A common pattern was for the chancel to be
enlarged, and then a west tower added to the older nave. A fifth of
the medieval churches have a 13th century tower, a high proportion
considering that half of the churches have no proper tower, only a
bellcote or timber belfry perched above the west gable of the nave.
Prior to the 1270s chancels are plain and simple with three lancet
windows in the east wall, and others in the north and south walls,
as at Kington. The towers are equally plain, and tend to be on the
short side. The towers of c1200-40 at Kington, Ledbury, Bosbury, and
Garway, plus those of c1260 and c1300 at Ewyas Harold and Richard's
Castle, are massive structures which may have had additional military
functions. All of them, and the tower of c1230 with a later timber
top at Holmer, are or were detached. In all England and Wales there
are only about 40 detached medieval belfries, and Herefordshire has
no less than seven which are detached as they now stand. Several
other towers, such as those in the two churches at Hereford, stand
on one side of the nave rather than in the usual position at the
west end. There are no surviving central towers of this period but
for one at Mordiford which was reduced to the height of the chancel
in c1812. Madley has a fine west tower which is embraced by aisles
running the full length of what was then the nave and chancel. The
porch at Clodock is an unusually early survival, and there is work
of note also at Walford-on-Wye, Much Marcle, and Dilwyn.

Bosbury, c1200-20

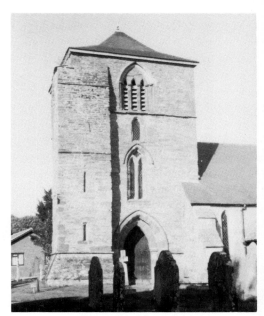

Ewyas Harold, c1260

St Weonards, c1520

Peterstow, 15th century

FOUR HEREFORDSHIRE CHURCH TOWERS

7

South side of Dilwyn Church.

THE 14th CENTURY

Towards the end of the 13th century the simple Early English style developed into the more florid and showy style known in England as Decorated. There is much work of the period 1290-1350 to be seen in the churches although by the 1320s it was increasingly a matter of completing, altering, extending, or repairing older structures rather than the building of totally new structures. There are many chancels of c1290-1320 and two dozen 14th century towers to add to those already built or begun by c1300. Spires are quite common in Herefordshire. Of those built of stone that at Withington may be as early as the 1290s, but the other notable examples at Stretton Grandison, Hereford, Goodrich, Llangarron, Ross, Weobley, Sellack, Stoke Edith, and Peterchurch are all of the 14th century. Some of these churches have other major portions of this period. The tower at Weobley was originally detached, and at Yarpole and Pembridge are low timber framed detached belfries. Of c1310-20 are the wide aisle at Leominster and the north chapel at Ledbury with huge four light windows studded with ballflowers, the apsed chancels at Madley and Marden, and almost all of the churches at Kingsland and Ashperton. The latter has shallow transepts, and most of those that exist in Herefordshire are of c1270-1340, as at Lyonshall, Mansell Gamage, Weobley, Bodenham, Pembridge, and Richard's Castle. At Leintwardine the considerable 14th century contributions include a large north chapel and a lofty SW porch-tower. Most of the smaller churches of Vowchurch, Pencoyd, and Huntingdon are also of this period, showing the Decorated style in a plainer and much more modest form.

THE 15th AND EARLY 16th CENTURIES

The late medieval building boom responsible for so much work in parish churches elsewhere in England hardly made any impression on those in Herefordshire. There are about a dozen stone towers, some timber belfries, a number of porches, both of stone and wood, a few inserted windows, and much internal woodwork, including roofs, but hardly any new aisles, transepts, or chantry chapels. The towers all stand at the west end except for that at Much Marcle. That at Linton, and the chapels at King's Capel, Sellack, and Bosbury have stone vaulted ceilings. Only one church, that of St Weonards with an early 16th century tower and north aisle, has more work of this period than of any other era.

LATER PERIODS

Rotherwas chapel was rebuilt in the 1580s but contains too much work of earlier and later periods to be of much significance. There are also four unimportant towers which are likely to be of c1530-1600. Between then and the Civil Wars of the 1640s the only work of note was the restoration of Abbey Dore. A new tower was added but the furnishings are much more important than the new building. Brampton Bryan church was wrecked by the Royalists during the wars and was entirely rebuilt except for the tower-arch in the 1650s as a wide single chamber covered with a hammerbeam roof. Of greater interest are the nave and chancel of 1679 at Monnington-on-Wye, and the tower, nave, and south transept of 1693 at How Caple.

When Norton Canon church was rebuilt in brick in 1718 the old windows and their glass were carefully preserved. Alterations have spoiled the original character of the churches built at Tyberton in 1719, and Preston Wynne in 1727. Neither is Whitney church, as rebuilt in 1740, of much interest. The work of 1740 at Stoke Edith, however, is memorable for the huge columns inside, not dividing off aisles, for none of these churches are aisled, but the east and west ends. By far the best church of this period is at Shobdon, as rebuilt in the Gothick style in the 1750s with ogival arches over the windows, and a full set of matching furnishings. Several older churches have 18th century towers, as at Eardisley and Eardisland, but none of these, or any other additions, are of much importance.

There is only one later 18th century church in Herefordshire, and the 19th century buildings do not concern us here. However it should be noted that no less than ten churches were enlarged with an added north aisle (and in one case a south aisle as well), and several towers, etc, were rebuilt, and many windows were renewed.

ROOFS

The earliest and the simplest form of church roof was the trussed rafter type, the framing of which usually looks seven sided from below. Herefordshire examples are difficult to date and the only specimen for which a date is known is that at Longtown, which was built as late as 1640. From the 14th century onwards there are many roofs with arched braces up to collar-beams with or without tie-beams below, king-posts or raking struts forming trefoils or quatre--foils above, and tiers of wind braces also forming quatrefoils. Coved roofs with bosses are rare in Herefordshire, but there is an example at Kenderchurch. Hammerbeam roofs are also uncommon, but occur at Hereford All Saints, 15th century, Holmer, c1500, Rotherwas Chapel, 1589, and Brampton Bryan, 1656.

The Bellhouse, Pembridge Church

The interior of Shobdon Church

THE DEVELOPMENT OF WINDOWS

Doorways and masonry styles can help to date the different parts
of old churches, but usually the shape and style of the windows is
the best evidence, although it should be borne in mind that they
may either be later insertions or earlier openings re-positioned.
During the 12th century windows gradually increased in size from
the tiny round headed windows of the Saxon and Early Norman periods
as at Bredwardine to the lancet windows with pointed heads which
appear in c1190-1200 at Holmer and Bosbury. Plain Norman windows
occur in dozens of churches. More ornate windows, like those with
nook-shafts and roll-moulded surrounds at Kilpeck of c1140 are rare.
Windows with two narrow lights under an outer arch occur in the
tower bell chambers at Fownhope and Eaton Bishop.

   Large lancets with and without nook-shafts occur at Abbey Dore
as early as c1200-20, and many early to mid 13th century chancels
such as Kington, Upton Bishop, and Weston-Under-Penyard. The usual
arrangement is a widely spaced group of three in the east wall and
even spaced single ones along the sides. The tower at Madley shows
pairs and triples of lancets more closely grouped. Probably of the
1260s are the trefoiled-headed lights in pairs at Bridge Sollars,
and the three lights under an outer arch in the tower bell-stage at
Ewyas Harold. Below the latter is a two light window with the space
between the heads pierced by a lozenge. By widening the lights and
making the subdividing mullions more delicate the Y-tracery typical
of c1300 is produced. Intersecting tracery, as at Much Marcle, is
the variant with three or more lights. Sometimes the arch heads and
lozenges of this type of tracery have cusps. Geometrical tracery
of the 1290s appears in the north aisle west window at Ledbury.

   A style which was peculiar to Herefordshire in c1295-1325 is
where there are three lights with the mullions rising straight up
to the arch-head with sharply pointed heads only to the lights on
each side, as at Much Marcle and Vowchurch. There are cinquefoiled
circles in windows of c1310-20 at Marden and Leominster, the latter
studded with ballflowers, but the curvilinear petal-like forms of
the Decorated style in other parts of England are hardly found at
all in Herefordshire. A common design of c1320-50 is reticulation,
or net-like tracery utilising the newly discovered ogival arch, as
at Madley, Llanwarne, and Almeley. The examples at Hampton Bishop
and Kinnersley with longer reticulation units are of c1360-1400.

   The motif already described of mullions rising straight up to
the main arch without interuption, with only minor subdivisions of
the lights between, is the hallmark of the Perpendicular style in
vogue from the late 14th century until the early 16th. Leominster
Priory has a huge west window of this type with two of the many
mullions taking the form of stepped buttresses. More typical is the
west window at Richard's Castle. On the whole, though, 15th century
windows in Herefordshire parish churches call for little comment.
The four-centered arch is used sometimes, as at Tarrington and in
the chapel of c1510 at Bosbury. Square headed two light windows
with the lights simply cusped, or even uncusped, are common.

   Unaltered windows of the late 16th, 17th, and 18th centuries
are rare in Herefordshire parish churches. Monington-On-Wye of 1769
has mullion-and-transom windows with segmental arches over all the
lights. The simple round arch is used in the 18th century as at
Stoke Edith. More exciting is the return of the ogival form for the
main arch and the heads of the lights at Shobden in the 1750s. The
Victorians experimented with all the older styles, and examples of
their period occur frequently in the churches. Some reproduce what
was there before, others ignore it, or are completely new openings.

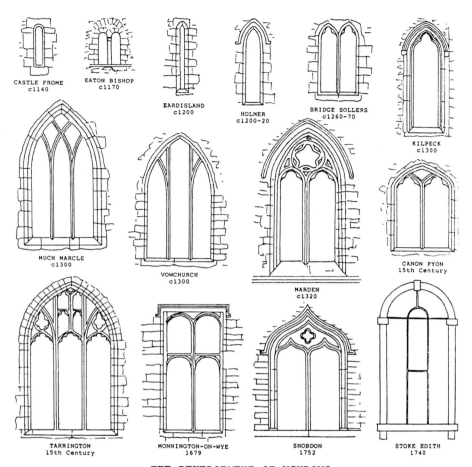

THE DEVELOPMENT OF WINDOWS

Labels within the figure:

CASTLE FROME c1140

EATON BISHOP c1170

EARDISLAND c1200

HOLMER c1200-20

BRIDGE SOLLERS c1260-70

KILPECK c1300

MUCH MARCLE c1300

VOWCHURCH c1300

MARDEN c1320

CANON PYON 15th Century

TARRINGTON 15th Century

MONNINGTON-ON-WYE 1679

SHOBDON 1752

STOKE EDITH 1740

FURNISHINGS

FONTS

Norman fonts are numerous in Herefordshire. Two dozen are noted as of interest in the gazetteer and there are many more which are not closely datable, being simple unadorned tubs. Apart from those of c1150-60 at Castle Frome and Eardisley by The Herefordshire School there are others of note at How Caple and Michaelchurch. There are several fonts of each of the medieval periods and a slightly later group of the 17th century. Lea has an Italian stoup of c1200 in use as a font. At Burghill a Norman font now serves as the base for a 13th century lead bowl with foliage. The 13th century font at Hope -under-Dinmore has arcading with figures, while the 14th century font at Weobley has panels on blank traceried windows. The badges and panelling at Fownhope are typically late medieval. Aston Ingham has a lead bowl dated 1689, and Credenhill a fluted bowl dated 1667.

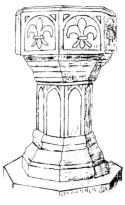

Font at Fownhope Church

Rood Loft, St Margarets

SCREENS

In the later medieval period it became customary for the chancels of churches to be divided off from the nave by a screen with a rood or image of the crucifixion set over it. Sometimes there was a loft over the screen used by musicians and the performers of religious plays. Other screens divided off side chapels and transepts. Some were ripped out during the Reformation of the mid 16th century when idols were banned and the priest's activities in the chancel were supposed to be more open to view, but simple screens without images were still being provided in the 17th century, as at Abbey Dore. The 19th century restorations saw many more removed, replaced, or cut down, but stairs giving access to the loft sometimes remain, as at Little Hereford and Pembridge. Two dozen churches have old screens or the remains of them. Welsh Newton has a very rare 14th century stone screen. Others of wood of c1400-1540 can be seen at Bosbury, Burghill, Aymestrey, and St Margarets.

OTHER FURNISHINGS AND FITTINGS

Medieval pulpits are rare as long sermons only became fashionable in the 16th century. Weobley has fragments of a 14th century stone pulpit, and there are others of the 15th century and c1530 of wood at Stretton Grandison and Wigmore. A few pulpits may be Elizabethan but by far the biggest group, apart from the Victorian ones, are of c1610-40. Some have classical motifs, such as arcading, pilasters, etc. Some medieval doors survive, and there are instances of old ironwork being re-used on later doors. A Norman doorknocker remains at Dormington. Some churches have communion rails around the altar table dating from the 16th, 17th, or 18th centuries. Late medieval tiles with heraldic designs survive in several churches. There is medieval glass at about 20 places, but single figures and fragments are more common than complete windows. Madley has some 13th century medallions, and part of a 14th century Jesse Tree, and other 14th century glass remains at Eaton Bishop, Dilwyn, and Credenhill. At Leintwardine and Hampton Bishop are remains of medieval reredoses of stone. Stalls fitted with miserichords (hinged seats with lips to support people when standing) remain at Leintwardine, St Peter's at Hereford, Holme Lacy and Canon Pyon, and late medieval bench ends remain in several other places. Originally each church possessed a lockable chest in which the plate was kept. Those at Kingstone, Garway, Orleton, and elsewhere are carved out of single trunks.

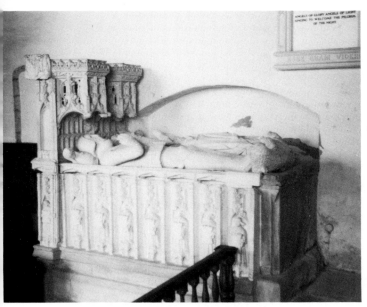

Croft: Tomb of St Richard Croft, d1509.

Tomb Chest at Bridstow Church

Coffin Lid at
Woolhope Church

MONUMENTS

PRE-REFORMATION MONUMENTS

There are four dozen effigies, four engraved brasses, five incised slabs inlaid with pitch, and three indents formerly filled with some sort of cement composition, surviving from before 1540 in the parish churches of Herefordshire. Two thirds, which is an unusually high proportion, are of the 13th and 14th centuries, and also of that period are the coffin lids with floriated crosses on them at about a dozen churches, and the plain shrine-like tomb chests at Goodrich and Bridstow. Sollars Hope has an incised slab of as early as c1225. There are rare oak effigies of c1300 and c1370 at Clifford and Much Marcle. The earliest effigies of stone are the ladies at Woolhope and Welsh Bicknor, and the knights at Abbey Dore, all late 13th century. There are notable effigies at Croft, Pembridge, Weobley, Kington, Ross, Ledbury, Much Marcle and Clehonger. The latter also has the best brass, which depicts a knight who died in 1483. Edvin Loach has four notable monuments of the period c1275-1340.

Coffin Lid at
Mansell Gamage

Brass of Joan Rudhall,
Brampton Abbotts Church

13

POST-REFORMATION MONUMENTS

Over 70 monuments of the period 1540-1700 survive, in addition to many plain inscriptions which are not noted in the gazetteer. The series of tomb chests with recumbent effigies on the lid continues until the Civil War period, as at Holme Lacy, 1571, Madley, 1575, Ross, 1635, and Much Marcle, 1650. Some effigies are set against a round arch, as at those of 1573 and 1578 at Bosbury, and kneeling couples set within arches are common, as at Much Dewchurch, 1625, and those of the 1630s at Ledbury and Kinnersley. At Bacton is a rustic monument showing one of Queen Elizabeth's maids of honour kneeling beside her. The few brasses of this period also usually show figures kneeling facing towards each other or an altar, as at Lugwardine, of 1622. 17th century clerics at Ledbury, Lugwardine, and Foy are shown as frontal demi-figures, often holding books. At Monnington in 1667 a mere bust suffices, but two Colonels of the Civil War are commemorated by full size statues at Ross and Weobley.

The emphasis on effigies decreased during the 17th century and eventually mural tablets with lengthy inscriptions became normal. Sometimes these have architectural surrounds, urns, cherubs, the symbols of death or of a profession, and other adornments. A dozen tablets of 1654 to 1714 have the twisted columns often used in the Baroque architectural style. Cast iron ledger stones with lettering only appear from 1619 to 1678 at Burrington, and also at Brilley.

Brass to Jane Best, Lugwardine Church

Ross-on-Wye: Colonel William Rudhall, d165

Kentchurch: John Scudamore, d1616

14

GAZETTEER OF OLD CHURCHES IN HEREFORDSHIRE

ABBEY DORE *St Mary*   SO 387304

Dore Abbey was a Cistercian monastery founded in 1147. A large new
cruciform church 75m long was built in c1175-90. It originally had
a two bay chancel flanked by pairs of one bay chapels opening off
the transepts, but the innermost chapels were absorbed into aisles
of a longer chancel with an eastern ambulatory built in c1200-20.
Cistercian churches rarely saw further use after the Dissolution,
but here, in the 1630s, Lord Scudamore had a new west wall built
to close off the decayed eastern parts for parochial use, and a
tower was raised above the south chancel aisle. The nave and other
buildings were abandoned and little now remains of any of them.
   The screen, stalls, benches, pulpit and tester, west gallery,
communion rail and some of the stained glass date from the 1630s.
There are also older fragments of glass, various sculptured stones
from the abbey buildings, 13th century heraldic tiles, two effigies
of 13th century knights, and a tomb chest of John Hoskins, d1638.

ACONBURY *St John The Baptist*   SO 517336

A convent of sisters of the Order of St John of Jerusalem founded
here in the 1230s was shortly afterwards transferred to Augustinian
canonesses, who built the present plain rectangular church in the
late 13th century. It has several original windows, a west doorway
with a timber porch, and two blocked south doorways which led to
the cloister. The east end has been shortened with old materials.
In a tomb recess of c1300 inside is a coffin lid with an incised
floriated cross and an inscription of Lombardic letters.

ACTON BEAUCHAMP *St Giles*   SO 680504

The short west tower with a pyramidal roof is probably medieval.
It has a south doorway the lintel of which is a re-set portion of
a finely carved 9th century cross-shaft with various creatures.
The nave and chancel were rebuilt in 1819 except for the late 12th
century south doorway with shafts and a roll-moulding in the arch.

■ 12th Century
▥ 13th Century
▧ 14th Century
▤ 16th Century

0 _____ 10
      Metres

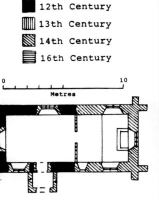

PLAN OF AMBERLEY CHURCH

Abbey Dore

Almeley Church

ALLENSMORE *St Andrew*   SO 467358

The south doorway is Late Norman but the nave and chancel were otherwise rebuilt in c1280-1300 and have several windows of that period. The east window with reticulated tracery and fragments of original glass must be of c1330, and the west tower, north doorway, and one north window are 15th century. The pulpit is Jacobean, and there is a large late 14th century incised slab to Sir Andrew Herl and his wife, and a tablet and scrolls to Richard Grumor, d1702.

ALMELEY *St Mary*   SO 332516

The short west tower was begun in c1200. The chancel dates from the end of the 13th century. It has a Geometrical east window, and a chancel arch supported on busts, with another bust at the apex. The tomb recess with an ogival top must be slightly later. The four bay aisles and the nave clerestory are early 14th century. The roof has a pretty ceilure with painted Tudor roses above the rood screen. The rood stair is 14th century. The tower arch screen is Jacobean.

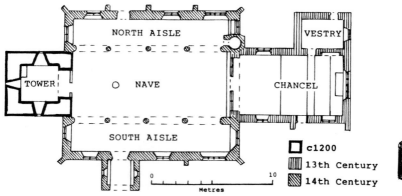

PLAN OF ALMELEY CHURCH

Font at Aston Ingram

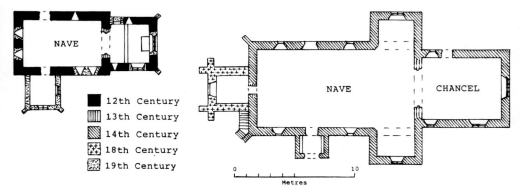

12th Century
13th Century
14th Century
18th Century
19th Century

PLAN OF ASTON CHURCH   PLAN OF ASHPERTON CHURCH

AMBERLEY *Dedication Unknown*   SO 546479

The nave masonry and the re-set porch outer entrance are Norman.
The rest, including the porch and double bellcote, is early 14th
century. Inside the east wall is a castellated 15th century frame.

ASHPERTON *St Bartholomew*   SO 643415

The chancel, wide unaisled nave, and small transepts are all early
14th century. Only the 13th century chancel arch is earlier. The
west tower was rebuilt in c1800. There is a tablet with columns and
a segmental pediment to a 17th century member of the Wilson family.

ASTON *St Giles*   SO 461718

The Norman nave has original north and south doorways but most of
the windows are renewed. The tympanum over the south doorway has a
lamb with a cross in a circle held by the bull of St Luke and the
eagle of St John, and an outer band with animals and foliage. The
nave has a roof with tie-beams, queen-posts, collar-beams and wind
braces. It probably dates from the 17th century.

ASTON INGRAM *St John The Baptist*   SO 693236

The church was mostly rebuilt by Nicholson & Son in 1891, excepting
only the south doorway and chancel arch of c1200, the 16th century
west tower within the nave, the lead font of 1689 with foliage and
initials, and two 13th century effigies set either side the altar.

AVENBURY *St Mary*   SO 661531

Little now remains of the nave, but the late 12th century chancel
and the early 13th century tower ruins lie among thick vegetation.

AYLTON *Dedication Unknown*   SO 658377

The Norman nave has one original north window. The south doorway,
the extension which forms the chancel, and the screen are all 14th
century. The south porch of 1654 with balusters, and the nave west
wall were rebuilt in the 18th and 19th centuries.

17

Aymestrey Church

The tympanum at Aston Church

Bacton: monument to Blanche Parry

AYMESTREY *St John The Baptist and St Alkmund*   SO 426651

The Norman chancel has two original north windows. The quatrefoil shaped arcade piers are also Norman. They are either re-set or have been brought in from elsewhere and given new capitals and arches. One suggested source for them is Wigmore Abbey, but the Norman nave there was aisleless, and the piers are not likely to have come from the domestic buildings. The west tower and the aisles are late 15th to early 16th century, and of c1530-40 is the fine rood screen with linenfold panelling in the dado and a coving with lierne ribs. The parclose screens are of the same date. The pulpit is Jacobean, and there is an incised alabaster slab to Sir John Lingen, d1506, and his wife, and a large classical style tablet with Doric pilasters to Robert Weever, d1728.

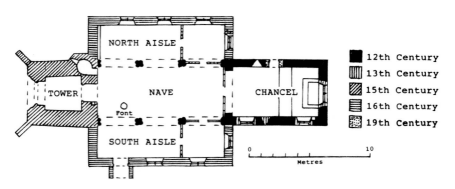

■	12th Century
|||||	13th Century
⧄	15th Century
▤	16th Century
▩	19th Century

NORTH AISLE

TOWER   NAVE   CHANCEL

Font

SOUTH AISLE

0   10
Metres

PLAN OF AYMESTREY CHURCH

BACTON *St Faith*   SO 371324

The tower was rebuilt in c1575 except for the 13th century tower
arch. The single bodied church is otherwise 15th century. The east
wall was rebuilt in 1894, although the window in it is original,
and the vestry and porch are also Victorian. The nave has a trussed
rafter roof, and the chancel has a wagon roof with bosses. Both are
15th century. The stalls are late medieval, and there is a fine 17th
century altar frontal. An interesting feature is a rustic monument
to Blanche Parry, maid of honour to Elizabeth I. Blanche is shown
kneeling beside the Queen. There is also a tablet to Alexander
Stanton, d1620, with kneeling figures shown facing each other.

BALLINGHAM *St Dubricius*   SO 576317

The nave has an early 13th century north lancet and a later 13th
century north window, while the south doorway and roof are 14th
century. The west tower is late 13th century, and the chancel and
rib vaulted south porch are 15th century. The pulpit is Jacobean
and there is a black and white tablet to William Scudamore, d1649.

BARTESTREE *St James*   SO 567409

A medieval chapel removed from Old Longworth now serves a convent.

BIRLEY *St Peter*   SO 454534

The Norman nave has an original south doorway and other windows of
the early and late 13th century. The chancel is 13th century but
the chancel arch is 14th century. The south chapel is late 14th
century with a later roof and timber framed gable. The west tower
was built in c1200 and has a pointed tower arch with early crocket
capitals. The Norman font has saltire crosses, arches, and a plait.

BISHOP'S FROME *St Mary*   SO 664484

The neo-Norman nave and north aisle are of 1861 and the chancel is
of 1847. Only the chancel arch with chevron ornament and the south
doorway with two orders of shafts with waterleaf capitals are real
12th century work. The west tower is 14th century, the screen is
partly old, and there is a late 13th century effigy of a knight
drawing his sword set in a later recess with ballflowers. A painted
monument to Margery de la Downes, d1598, has two kneeling figures
and a skeleton below, along with many interesting inscriptions.

BISHOPSTONE *St Lawrence*   SO 417438

There is a blocked Norman window in the nave south wall. The west
windows also look Norman but the whole wall is 14th century, as are
several other windows and the timber south porch which has been
transferred here from Yazor old church. The transepts and chancel
are 13th century. There are panels of foreign 16th and 17th century
glass in a south window, and in the north transept are recumbent
effigies of John Berinton, d1614, and his wife.

BLAKEMERE *St Leonard*   SO 362411

The church was rebuilt in 1877 and the internal facing is all of
that period, but the south doorway and chancel arch are of c1200
The priest's doorway and a chancel north window also appear Late
Norman, the chancel east wall has 13th century lancets, and there
are several other later medieval windows. The Norman font has a
rope moulding at the foot of the bowl, and the pulpit is Jacobean.

BODENHAM *St Michael* SO 530509

The west tower was begun in the late 13th century. It was finished
in the 14th century with a pyramidal roof set over the stump of an
incomplete recessed spire. The four bay arcades, wide aisles, porch,
and the chancel are all 14th century. The latter was shortened in
c1750. the east corners of the 13th century nave survive. The east
bays of the aisle form transepts and have end windows of the late
14th or 15th century. The 16th century clerestory includes re-set
14th century windows. The doorways have ballflowers. There is also
a 14th century female effigy with a child standing by her side.

BOLLINGHAM *St Silas* SO 302527

The 19th century rebuilding left only the original south walls and
the roof with tie-beams, king-posts, and collar-beams.

BOLSTONE *Dedication Unknown* SO 552327

Although mostly rebuilt in 1877 this little used chapel has Norman
doorways, two east windows of c1200, and two later south windows.
The Jacobean font has fleur-de-lis, a thistle, and a flower on it.

BOSBURY *Holy Trinity* SO 695435

The aisled nave with six bay arcades and the chancel represent a
substantial church of c1180-1200. Most of the lancet windows have
pointed heads, but the west window and doorways are round arched.
The large detached tower is 13th century, and the eastern bay of
the south aisle was rebuilt as a chapel in c1510 by Thomas Morton,
whose initials appear on the vaulted ceiling. There is also a large
19th century vestry. The font of c1200 stands on five columns. The
screen is medieval, the pulpit and reader's desk contain 16th and
17th century woodwork, and the lectern is Jacobean. In the south
aisle is a 14th century coffin lid with a foliated cross and two
other crosses. In the chancel are monuments to John Harford, d1573,
and Richard Harford, d1578, and his wife.

Bosbury Church

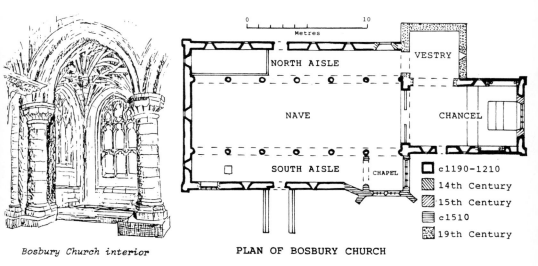

Bosbury Church interior

PLAN OF BOSBURY CHURCH

NORTH AISLE

VESTRY

NAVE

CHANCEL

SOUTH AISLE

CHAPEL

0 _____ 10
Metres

☐ c1190-1210
▨ 14th Century
▨ 15th Century
▤ c1510
▨ 19th Century

BRAMPTON ABBOTTS *St Michael*   SO 602265

The nave and chancel are both Norman. The south doorway and chancel arch each have one order of shafts, although the arch of the latter is a 16th century rebuild. The nave roof is 14th century, and the font is 15th century. There is a brass of Joan Rudhall, c1520. The figures of her husband John, d1507, and children are now missing.

Brampton Abbotts Church

BRAMPTON BRYAN *St Barnabas*   SO 370725

As rebuilt in 1656 for Sir Robert Harley, using some older walling,
the church has a short single chamber of great width corresponding
to the width of the medieval nave and aisle. It is covered by a
double hammerbeam roof. The pulpit has 17th century panels. A 14th
century effigy of a lady holding her heart in her hands lies in a
recess with 14th and 15th century tiles in the chancel south wall,
and there is a large monument to the 2nd Earl of Oxford, d1724.

BREDWARDINE *St Andrew*   SO 335445

The Early Norman nave has four original windows, tufa quoins, and
north and south doorways with large lintels carved with rosettes
and strange looking deities. The space once occupied by an apse
was later taken into the nave, and a new chancel, inclined to the
north, was built beyond to the east in c1300. The north tower was
added in 1790. There is a large plain Norman font, and on either
side of the altar are effigies of knights of the late 14th century
and c1450 respectively.

BREINTON *St Michael*   SO 474395

Only the west doorway of c1200, parts of three Norman west windows,
a 14th century chancel window, and a little masonry on the south
side, survived the building of 1866-70 by R.F.Kempson. Inside is a
rustic painted tablet to Captain Rudhall Booth, d1685.

Bridge Sollers Church

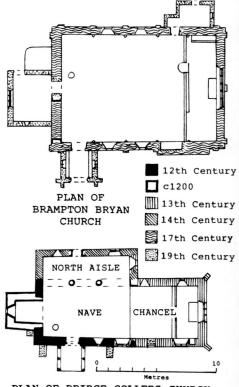

PLAN OF
BRAMPTON BRYAN
CHURCH

■ 12th Century
□ c1200
▥ 13th Century
▨ 14th Century
▧ 17th Century
▦ 19th Century

NORTH AISLE

NAVE   CHANCEL

0   10
Metres

PLAN OF BRIDGE SOLLERS CHURCH

Brobury Church, now a house.

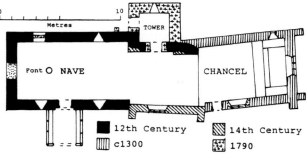

BREDWARDINE CHURCH

BRIDGE SOLLERS *St Andrew*   SO 415426

The Norman nave has an original south window and a doorway with the outer arch carried on a head with two dragons emanating from the mouth, and a dragon in profile. The west tower is also 12th century and the two eastern bays of the arcade are of c1180. The west bay of the aisle itself and the chancel are early 14th century.

BRIDSTOW *St Bridget*   SO 585249

Only the Norman chancel arch with chevrons, the 13th century two bay arcade to a north chapel, and the 15th century tower survived the rebuilding by T. Nicholson in 1862. A 13th century tomb chest with cusped arches on colonettes lies in a recess in the chancel.

BRILLEY *St Mary*   SO 260493

The thin west tower is of 1912, the chancel was rebuilt in 1890, and the nave windows are renewed, but the transeptal north chapel dates from c1300, and the nave and chancel roofs are old. That over the nave has tie-beams, one of which has cusped raking struts and a cusped collar. There are two cast-iron slabs of 1669-70.

BRIMFIELD *St Michael*   SO 526675

The Norman west tower has a timber framed top stage, probably 17th century. The nave and chancel were rebuilt in the 19th century.

BRINSOP *St George*   SO 442448

The single chamber nave and chancel with a four bay arcade to a north aisle are mostly of c1300-50, but the chancel has some older walling. There are wall paintings of c1300 and c1330 showing the Annunciation and Visitation, and the Crucifixion, two coffin lids with foliated crosses, a very fine tympanum of c1150-60 depicting St George, other Norman sculptured fragments, a 15th century stoup, an old screen, and a tablet to William Dansey, d1708.

BROBURY *St Mary Magdalene*   SO 345443

The nave was demolished in 1853, and the chancel of c1300 with a re-set later tomb recess, and a 17th century roof, now forms a house.

BROCKHAMPTON-BY-BROMYARD *Dedication Unknown*   SO 686560

West of Lower Brockhampton House is a ruined single chamber chapel with windows of c1200, the 13th century, and the late 14th century.

BROCKHAMPTON-BY-ROSS *Holy Trinity*   SO 597317

The ruined old church by Brockhampton Court Hotel is probably 13th century. Two windows are 15th century, and the west tower and south porch are late 16th century. The new church to the NW is of 1901.

23

The north side of Bromyard Church

BROMYARD *St Peter* SO 656548

Of a cruciform Norman church there remains the masonry of the nave
west wall, the transepts, and the splendid re-set north and south
doorways with three orders of shafts, and lozenges, rosettes and
chevrons on the arches. Aisles with five bay arcades were added on
the south and north in c1190 and c1210 respectively. The piers were
heightened in 1805. In the early 14th century the crossing arches
were renewed, and a new tower built above them, a long new chancel
was built, and the aisles were widened to project as far as the
transepts. The many tomb recesses both inside and out are also of
that era, while the north transept end window is slightly earlier.
The buttresses, vestry, and the windows of the chancel and western
facade are Victorian. There is a Norman panel with a relief of St
Peter above the south doorway, and the font with chevrons, a tree
of life, and a running scroll motif, is also Norman. In the church
is a metal bushel of 1670 which was once used as a legal measure.

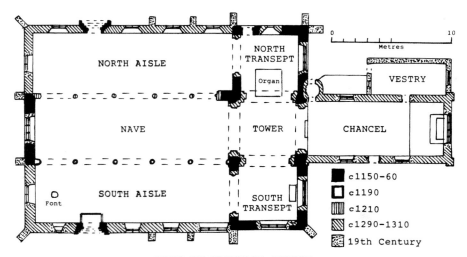

PLAN OF BROMYARD CHURCH

BURGHILL *St Mary*   SO 480445

There is a re-set Norman doorway between the wide chancel and the
vestry of the 14th century, and a Norman window close by. In c1200
aisles were added to the nave, but only the south aisle end walls,
a north aisle end wall, and the west respond of the north arcade, have
survived the replacement of the five bay arcades in the early 13th
and 14th centuries, and a very heavy restoration of 1880. The tower
was rebuilt in 1812. The stem and the rim of the lead bowl of the
font are of c1200, the pulpit is Jacobean, and there is a medieval
screen with a coving deep enough to require support from a pair of
Jacobean posts. The communion rail is late 17th century. On a tomb
chest are recumbent effigies of Sir John Milbourne and his wife,
c1440, and there is a brass inscription and globe commemorating the
traveller Robert Masters, d1619.

BURRINGTON *St George*   SO 443721

The church was mostly rebuilt in the 1850s. Outside to the east are
six cast-iron slabs dating from 1619-78. One is to Richard Knight,
d1645. His family probably produced the slabs at Bridgnorth.

BYFORD : *St John The Baptist*   SO 397429

The eastern part of the nave, with one original north window, and
the western part of the chancel, formed the original Norman church.
A three bay south aisle was added in c1190. Two more bays to the
west, a new south doorway, and a square south chapel with a two bay
arcade, were added in the 13th century. The chancel was doubled in
length in c1300, and the windows and wall-painting of St Margaret
in the south chapel, and the south porch are 14th century. The font
dated 1638 has four badges on it. The tower was added in 1717.

BYTON *St Mary*   SO 371642

The hill-top church of 1859-60 has a Norman font with chevrons and
against the south wall a Norman tympanum with the Lamb and cross.

CALLOW *St Mary*   SO 490344

In the church of 1830, altered in 1884, is a 14th century font.

CANON FROME *St James*   SO 645435

The church lies beside Canon Frome Court. It was entirely rebuilt
in 1860 by Bodley, except for the brick west tower of 1680.

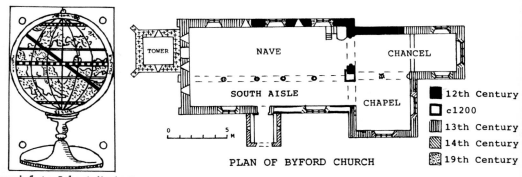

*Memorial to Robert Masters,
Burghill Church*

PLAN OF BYFORD CHURCH

■	12th Century
□	c1200
▥	13th Century
▨	14th Century
▨	19th Century

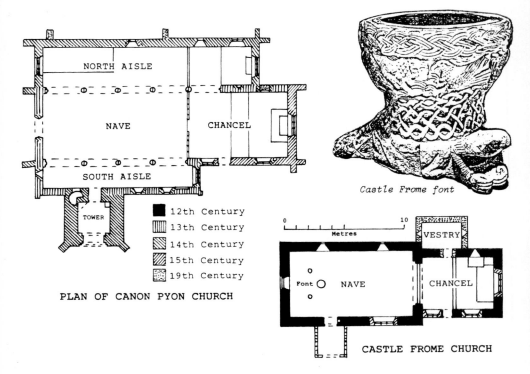

North Aisle · Nave · Chancel · South Aisle · Tower

- ■ 12th Century
- ▥ 13th Century
- ▨ 14th Century
- ▧ 15th Century
- ▦ 19th Century

PLAN OF CANON PYON CHURCH

Castle Frome font

VESTRY · Font · NAVE · CHANCEL

0 — 10 Metres

CASTLE FROME CHURCH

CANON PYON *St Lawrence*   SO 450492

The wide nave and chancel are undivided except by an old screen. The dramatically leaning north and south arcades of the early and late 13th century respectively were originally both of four bays but an extra bay to serve a new north chapel was added in the 14th century, when the aisle was widened and the old east respond was re-set. Most of the windows and the porch tower on the south side are 14th century, and the east window and priest's door are 15th century. The tower helps to support the south arcade by means of flying buttresses. The 15th century font has a quatrefoil frieze, and there are stalls with miserichords carved with various animals. The indents of a couple of c1400 were filled with a sort of cement composition, and there is a monument to George Sawyer, d1753.

CASTLE FROME *St Michael*   SO 667459

The Early Norman nave and chancel have several original windows and a west doorway with a blank tympanum. Two south windows, the east window, and the chancel ceilure with panels, diagonal ribs, and some bosses, are 15th century, while the pretty timber framed bell turret and south porch date from a sensitive restoration of 1878 by Martin Buckle. Inside is a particularly fine font of c1170 carved with the Baptism of Christ, the signs of the Evangelists, and two doves. The pulpit has some plain late 17th century panels, whilst the stalls have Jacobean arches on the fronts, there are old tiles in the back of the piscina, and in a nave south window some 15th century glass. Re-set in a chancel window is a small bust of a knight holding what appears to be his heart. There is also a tomb chest with recumbent alabaster effigies of c1630, and a tablet to Frances Unett, d1656.

Clodock Church

CLEHONGER *All Saints*　　　　　　　　　　　　SO 466378

Relics of the Norman church are the nave west window now looking
into an early 13th century tower, the re-set south doorway with
a keeled roll-moulding and colonettes with waterleaf capitals, and
the stone with chevron re-used in the south wall of the chancel of
c1300. The four bay south arcade is mid-13th century whilst the
aisle itself has windows with Y-tracery of c1300. Another window
of that period is re-used in the north chapel built by Sir Richard
Pembrugge to serve a chantry he founded in 1341, and to contain his
very fine effigy. The smaller effigy of a lady may be his widow.
Also in the chapel are brasses to Sir John Barre, d1483, and his
wife, and there is part of a 13th century coffin lid with the usual
foliated cross, and a tablet to Herbert Aubrey, d1671, and wife.

CLIFFORD *St Mary*　　　　　　　　　　　　SO 252450

The church lies in woods far from the village. The priest's doorway
and the round arched recess in the chancel are Norman. Otherwise,
the chancel is early 13th century, the nave is late 13th century,
the west tower is 18th century with older material, and the north
aisle is of 1887. Inside is an oak effigy of c1300.

CLODOCK *St Clodock*　　　　　　　　　　　　SO 327275

The large nave has two Norman north windows and a wide chancel arch
of c1190. The chancel was rebuilt in the 13th century, and given a
new east window in c1300. The west tower and three south windows
are 15th century, and there is a 16th century window in the chancel.
The porch may be as early as c1200. There are pews dated 1660, 1668,
and 1701, a three decker pulpit and tester, stalls of 1657, a west
gallery of c1715, and an inscribed 9th century tombstone.

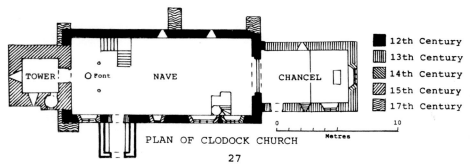

■	12th Century
▥	13th Century
▨	14th Century
▧	15th Century
▨	17th Century

PLAN OF CLODOCK CHURCH

27

CODDINGTON *All Saints*   SO 718427

The round headed doorways suggest a date of c1200 but the nave and chancel both have several 13th century lancets, and a dedication of three altars took place in 1231. The nave roof with collar-beams on arched braces forming two-centered arches could also be of the 13th century. The west tower with a broach spire was built in 1865 by Kempson, and the porch and vestry are also Victorian.

COLLINGTON *St Mary*   SO 449601

A 13th century font with arches on colonettes lies in the church built in 1856 by A.E.Perkins.

COLWALL *St James*   SO 739423

The Late Norman south doorway has colonettes with trumpet scallop capitals. The south aisle with a five bay arcade is 13th century. Projecting south from the west end of the aisle is a tower begun in the 14th century, but with a 15th century top. The nave has a fine old roof with collar-beams on arched braces and two tiers of wind-braces. The existing chancel was built in 1865 by Woodyer, and the north aisle was added in 1880. The pulpit and tester are 17th century. In the north aisle is a 13th century tile showing one of the labours of the months, and in the south aisle is the brass of Elizabeth Hardord, d1590.

CRADLEY *St James*   SO 736471

The tower arch suggests that the large tower was built in c1200, and the chancel and nave doorways are Late Norman. The latter has colonettes and a chevron pattern. The chancel was rebuilt in 1868, and the large nave was rebuilt and provided with a narrow five bay north aisle in 1869. The rustic baluster font is of 1722. The old chest is unusually long. The stalls are partly 15th century and the timber framed lychgate is also medieval. On the north wall of the tower is a short re-set length of Saxon frieze and two small 17th century figures from a monument. The porch was added in 1893.

Colwall Church

Croft Church

Craswall Church

CRASWALL *St Mary* SO 281363

This remotely sited single-cell building, with the western portion walled off to form a lobby in the 18th century, has a 13th century priest's doorway, a 14th century east window, and a 15th century main doorway. The belfry is partly old and there is a seat outside the south and east walls. The other features are of later date.

CREDENHILL *St Mary* SO 450439

The nave has two 13th century north windows. The narrow chancel arch is early 13th century and is flanked by Victorian side-arches. The present chancel and the west tower are 14th century, and the tall timber porch is 15th century. The nave roof is old and has an alternating pattern of tie-beams and collar-beams and a series of arched wind braces. The font is dated 1667, and there is some 14th century glass in a chancel window, and shields in a nave window.

CROFT *St Michael* SO 451654

The church lies in front of the castle. It has a nave and chancel of c1300 with Y-tracery in the windows, and a 17th century bell turret with miniture balusters and an ogee cap covered in lead. The late 17th century north doorway has an oval window over it. Against the chancel are remains of a chapel which once housed the monument of Sir Richard Croft, d1509, and his wife. There are box pews, an early 18th century west gallery and medieval tiles, one dated 1456.

CUSOP *St Mary* SO 240415

Although much restored, the nave is Norman with a blocked doorway with a huge lintel on the north side, an original south window, a plain chancel arch, and a contemporary font with saltire crosses and a trellis of lozenges. The chancel may be Norman too, but has two 13th century lancet windows in the side walls.

Dilwyn Church

DEWSALL *St Michael*   SO 486335

Most of the features of the single chamber, including the timber porch, and the font with ballflowers, are of about the time of the consecration recorded in 1340.

DILWYN *St Mary*   SO 415547

The original Norman nave lay where the south aisle and southern half of the nave now are. For there is a big west tower of c1200 in line with this part, and the tower arch is partly blocked to provide an abutment for the five bay south arcade. Both the arcades, and the rest of the nave, aisles, and chancel, are late 13th century. The north transept and the tomb recess with ballflowers in the chancel are of c1310-30, whilst the south porch is still later. The rood screen and parclose screens are old, and in the south aisle are several coffin lids with foliated crosses and some 14th century tiles. Within the chancel is the effigy of a knight of c1320, and a 15th century indent with figures of a couple under canopies. It was filled with a type of cement or composition stone rather than the more usual cut-out sheets of brass.

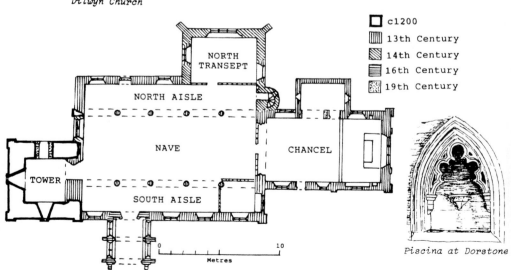

☐	c1200
▥	13th Century
▧	14th Century
▤	16th Century
▦	19th Century

Piscina at Dorstone

PLAN OF DILWYN CHURCH

DINEDOR *St Andrew*   SO 534367

The short nave and chancel are of 1867-8 by Kempson but the west
tower with a pyramidal roof has medieval masonry.

DINMORE *St John of Jerusalem*   SO 487504

A preceptory of the Knights of St John of Jerusalem was founded at
Dinmore in 1189. The Manor stands on the site of the preceptory
buildings and the chapel doorway towards it is Norman. The rest of
the present chapel, which originally was longer, is 14th century.
The west tower has a recessed spire.

DOCKLOW *St Bartholomew*   SO 564575

The west tower with a truncated pyramidal roof may be early 13th
century, and the single chamber nave and chancel may be later 13th
century, although the latter was mostly rebuilt by the Victorians.

DONNINGTON *St Mary*   SO 708343

The nave and chancel are probably of c1300, but the features are all
renewed, and a north aisle was added in 1862. Inside is a monument
to E.H.Webb, d1655, with an inscription on drapery.

DORMINGTON *St Peter*   SO 583402

The nave and chancel are probably 13th century, the chancel arch
being of that date, but most of the windows were renewed in 1877,
when the vestry and porch were added. More important is the Norman
door knocker in the shape of a feline head. On the west wall is a
faint wall painting of Christ in Majesty, and there are tablets to
Margaret Carpenter, d1666, and John Brydges, d1669.

DORSTONE *St Faith*   SO 315418

The church was much restored in 1889. The chancel of c1300 has a
double piscina with dogtooth ornament, and two original windows,
plus another of the 15th century. The tower arch is 13th century.

DOWNTON-ON-THE-ROCK *St Giles*   SO 428475

The old church ruin by the village has a narrow Norman chancel arch,
two late 13th century chancel windows, and a 14th century window
in the nave. The east and west end walls are 19th century rebuilds.

DULAS *St Michael*   SO 372294

Reassembled fragments of a Norman doorway from the old church form
a garden gate north of Dulas Court. In the new church of 1865 are
a pulpit, lectern, desk, and chairs, all 17th century work.

EARDISLAND *St Mary*   SO 421585

The long nave has several early 13th century windows and doorways,
the latter possibly re-positioned. The porch and the two recesses
for effigies are early 14th century. The chancel has sedilia and
other features of c1300, and the vestry is contemporary. The tower
was rebuilt in the 18th century. Under the Victorian tower arch is
an old screen. In the nave is a 15th century incised slab with a
foliated cross under an ogee canopy.

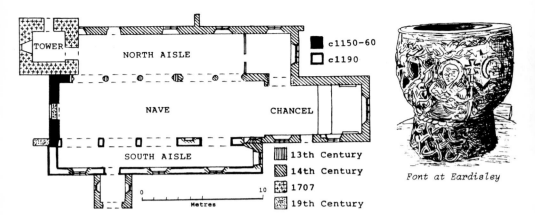

c1150-60
c1190

13th Century
14th Century
1707
19th Century

0   10
Metres

PLAN OF EARDISLEY CHURCH

Font at Eardisley

EARDISLEY   *St Mary Magdalene*   SO 313491

It would seem that the present nave constituted the whole of the
Norman church. At the end of the 12th century a narrow south aisle
and chapel were added with three arches towards the nave and just
one towards the chancel. Between the two is a solid length of wall
with a 14th century recess in it. In the 13th century a three bay
north aisle was added. A new chancel beyond the original one was
built in c1300 and a north chapel with a two bay arcade towards the
original chancel followed in the early 14th century. The south porch
and south aisle windows are also 14th century. The tower at the
west end of the north aisle was rebuilt in 1707.

In addition to its fascinating architectural history Eardisley
church has a very fine and important Norman font of c1160. There
are knot patterns on the stem, while the bowl has a plaited band at
the top and below a frieze of scenes, figures, and ornamentation
mixed up with no divisions between them. The chief scenes show two
knights in combat and the Harrowing of Hell with Christ frantically
pulling a man out of a maze of tentacle-like twisted knots. There
is also a splendid lion with long claws. There are two helms of
the 15th and 16th centuries in the nave.

EASTNOR   *St John*   SO 731372

The whole church was rebuilt by Sir G.G.Scott in 1852 except for
the 14th century west tower, the Norman south doorway and eastern
respond of the north arcade, and the 13th century piers and arches
of the arcade. There are many 18th and 19th century monuments.

EATON BISHOP   *St Michael*   SO 443391

The oblong west tower with two-light bell-openings is Norman. The
broach spire is a later addition. The four bay arcades and narrow
aisles are early 13th century, the NE window of the north aisle and
the chancel are of c1300, and the SE window in the south aisle is
slightly later. There are good reasons to believe that the very
fine stained glass in several windows dates from c1330 and was paid
for by Adam de Murimonth, Canon of Hereford, Cantor of Exeter from
1328. There is also a tablet to Richard Sneade, d1714.

EDVIN LOACH *St Mary*   SO 663585

East of the new church are ruins of the old church. It has an Early
Norman south doorway with herringbone masonry to the east. The east
end is 13th century, and the thin west tower is 16th century.

EDVIN RALPH *St Michael*   SO 645575

The nave and chancel form a single chamber. Both are Norman but the
chancel, with one original window, may be slightly later. The nave
has original doorways. Two fine monuments with effigies of a late
13th century husband and wife, and an early 14th century husband
and two wives of the Edefin family formerly lay in recesses in the
chancel but are now under the 13th century tower along with a tiny
female effigy and an incised slab to Maud de Edefen, d1325.

ELTON *St Mary*   SO 457710

The small Norman nave-and-chancel church by the Hall has original
doorways and one window. Other windows are 13th century and of the
restoration of 1876. There is a Jacobean pulpit, a screen with 15th
and 17th century parts, and Queen Elizabeth I's arms carved in wood.

EVESBATCH *St Andrew*   SO 687482

The chancel and most of the nave windows are of 1877, but the nave
is 14th century with a doorway and window of that date. The font
cover is Jacobean, and there are some late medieval bench ends. Two
females of the Dobyns family, d1658 and 1710, are commemorated by
monuments, the former being a frontal demi-figure holding a baby.

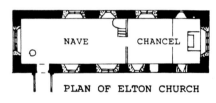

PLAN OF ELTON CHURCH

■ 12th Century
□ c1190-1200
▦ 13th Century
▧ 14th Century
▨ 15th Century
▒ 19th Century

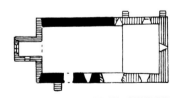

PLAN OF EDVIN LOACH CHURCH

0 ———————— 10
Metres

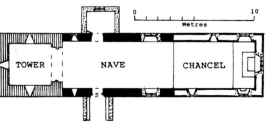

PLAN OF EDVIN RALPH CHURCH

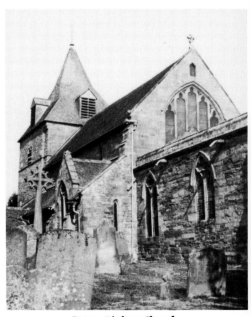

Eaton Bishop Church

33

EWYAS HAROLD *St Michael*   SO 387287

The 13th century west tower has a clasping stair turret at the SW corner and a south doorway. The tower arch dates from 1868, when the nave was rebuilt except for the thick walling below the north windows and the roof. The chancel of c1300 has an effigy of a lady holding her heart set in a tomb recess. The pulpit is Jacobean.

EYE *St Peter and St Paul*   SO 497638

The south aisle with a three bay arcade and parts of the chancel date from c1190 while the north aisle is of c1210-20. The chancel has a late 13th century north chapel and a 16th century east window. the nave clerestory of quatrefoil windows in niches and the tie-beam roof may be 14th century and the timber north porch is late 14th century. The west tower was mostly rebuilt in 1874. The pulpit looks Jacobean but is dated 1681, and there are benches with dolphin panels dated 1684. There are recumbent alabaster effigies on tomb chests of Sir Rowland Cornewall, d1520, and Sir Richard Cornewall, and his wife, c1540. The latter has Early Renaissance features.

EYTON *All Saints*   SO 475616

The single chamber has one Norman and one 14th century window and is divided by a fine screen of c1500 with a panelled loft coving. The other windows and vestry are Victorian.

FAWLEY *St John*   SO 591295

The Norman nave and the chancel of 1827 are connected by a narrow arch flanked by Victorian openings. The nave south wall is a thin rebuild probably of the 14th century, the date of the roof. There are fragments of an old screen, and a Norman font decorated with scallops which are probably re-cut.

FELTON *St Michael*   SO 579485

Although mostly rebuilt in 1853, and provided with a spire in 1891, the church has old material in the nave, chancel, and west tower.

FORD *Dedication Unknown*   SO 512553

The small nave and apse of 1851 may be built on Norman foundations.

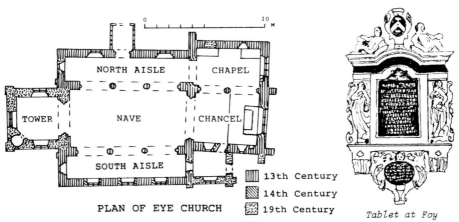

▓	13th Century
▨	14th Century
▥	19th Century

PLAN OF EYE CHURCH

Tablet at Foy

FOWNHOPE *St Mary*   SO 582343

The Norman central tower still has original belfry windows and arches to the east and west with chevrons. The tower north wall has 13th and 14th century windows. Also 14th century are the broach spire, the south aisle and chapel, the nave north windows (one has a Norman rere-arch, and the western arch of the arcade. The other two bays, plus the west end of the nave, and the north doorway, with two orders of shafts, are 13th century. The chancel with Y- and intersecting window tracery is of c1300. There are two tomb recesses, that with ballflowers being of c1310-30. The fonts are of c1670 and the 18th century. There is a loose tympanum of c1150 showing a lion with the Virgin and Child, an incised slab with many inscriptions, and tablets to Johanna Lechmere, d1692, Nicholas Lechmere, d1711, and John Kidley.

FOY *St Mary*   SO 597284

The nave north doorway and chancel north window are 13th century. The west tower, the cusped recess of an altar beside the chancel arch, the south porch, and most of the windows are 14th century. Following the terms of John Abrahall's will of 1640, the east window is a copy of that at Sellack. His initials and the year 1673 appear on the gable, and the glass, also copied from Sellack, is dated 1675.

Fownhope Church: The Spire

The pulpit, screen, communion rail, and stalls all incorporate 17th century work, whilst the south door is 14th century. In the chancel and the nave altar recess are two defaced late 13th century effigies with round objects at their feet. There are tablets to various Abrahalls, George, d1673, Paul, d1675, and John, d1702.

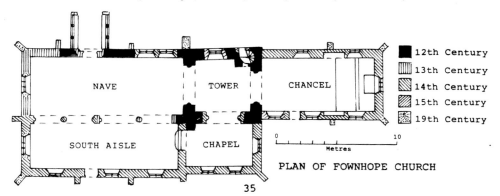

PLAN OF FOWNHOPE CHURCH

- ■ 12th Century
- ▥ 13th Century
- ▧ 14th Century
- ▨ 15th Century
- ▦ 19th Century

35

GARWAY *St Michael*

This church is unusually interesting. In the 1180s a preceptory of
the Templars was founded here, and excavations have laid bare the
foundations of a round nave built in imitation of Holy Sepulchre
church at Jerusalem. The chancel arch with two orders of colonettes
and chevrons on the arch, and part of the north wall of a chancel
which was probably apsed, also survive. The existing nave, the two
bay arcade to a south chapel, and the east part of the chancel are
late 13th century. The chapel itself, and the chancel east wall,
were rebuilt in the 16th century. The chancel roof with tie-beams,
collar beams, and two tiers of pointed trefoiled wind-braces, may
also be 16th century. A 17th century passageway-cum-porch connects
the nave to an early 13th century NW tower which was once detached
and perhaps intended as a military strongpoint. Sculptured panels
set on the outside of the nave are post-medieval. There are massive
16th or 17th century benches, stalls and panelling with Jacobean
work, and a 17th century communion rail.

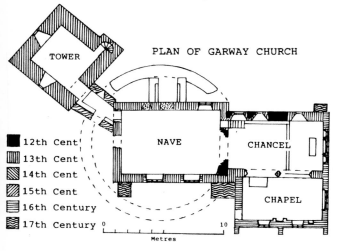

PLAN OF GARWAY CHURCH

■ 12th Cent
▦ 13th Cent
▧ 14th Cent
▨ 15th Cent
▤ 16th Century
▩ 17th Century

0   10

Metres

TOWER

NAVE

CHANCEL

CHAPEL

Hampton Bishop Church

*Garway
Church*

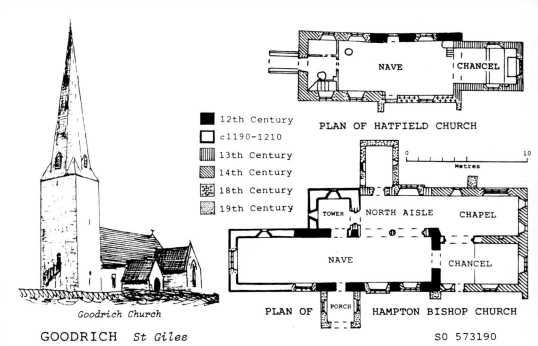

12th Century
c1190-1210
13th Century
14th Century
18th Century
19th Century

PLAN OF HATFIELD CHURCH

PLAN OF HAMPTON BISHOP CHURCH

Goodrich Church

GOODRICH *St Giles*   SO 573190

The church looks humble compared with the fine castle some distance
away. The nave and chancel form a single chamber. The middle two
bays of the six bay arcade are 13th century and the ends represent
a lengthening in c1300. The thin west tower and broach spire, and
south porch are 14th century, and the east window is 15th century.
Inside the church is a very damaged 13th century tomb chest.

GRAFTON *St Peter*   SO 510371

A tablet to John Daubeney, d1741, from the ruined old church with
a Norman north doorway, lies in the church of 1880 by Kempson.

GRENDON BISHOP *St John The Baptist*   SO 597564

This isolated church of 1787 in the fields was remodelled and given
an apse in 1870. A Norman window is re-set in the tower south wall.

HAMPTON BISHOP *St Andrew*   SO 558380

The Norman nave has a south doorway with a large lintel with scale
decoration and saltire crosses, a blank tympanum, an arch covered
with chevrons, and a hoodmould with billets. Of c1190-1200 are the
western extension of the nave, the north tower, and an arch between
the chancel and north chapel. The latter are otherwise of c1300.
East of the tower is a 13th century aisle with a two bay arcade. In
the chapel is a medieval reredos. The pulpit is partly Jacobean.

HATFIELD *St Leonard*   SO 586594

The Early Norman nave north wall of herringbone masonry has a door-
-way with a tympanum decorated with a trellis pattern. The chancel
is 13th century, and the western part of the nave, now forming a
lobby with a bell turret above, is 14th century. Part of the south
wall is 17th century, and there are tablets of 1641, 1669, & 1673.

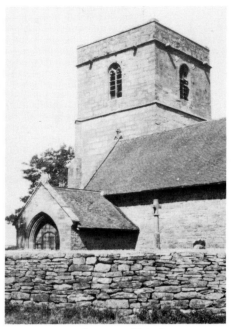

All Saints' Church, Hereford   *Holme Lacy Church*

HENTLAND *St Dubricius*   SO 543264

The nave, chancel, and north aisle with a four bay arcade all have features of c1300-50, whilst the west tower is late 14th century, but the whole was much restored in 1853 by Seddon, and the vestry and north porch are Victorian. The font is 15th century and so are the three stained glass figures in the east window.

HEREFORD *All Saints*   SO 508401

The oldest part of the church is the eastern respond of an early 13th century north aisle arcade exposed behind the respond of the present late 13th century arcade. So before 1300 the aisle had been rebuilt wider, given a large tower to the west, and a chapel to the east. The south aisle and arcade are also late 13th century. Here the eastern respond was moved westwards in the 15th century when a stair turret to the rood loft was provided on this side. In the 14th century the south chapel was greatly enlarged and in the late 14th century the chancel was given a new east window, and probably still later its wagon roof with bosses. The south aisle also has later 14th century windows and a shallow porch of that period has been transferred from the aisle to the south chapel. The north aisle has a hammerbeam roof for which the nave clerestory has been abolished on the north side.
There are 14th century stalls with miserichords carved with various figures and creatures and a fine contemporary chest. The pulpit is an ornate piece, dated 1621. In the south chapel is a reredos of c1700 with fluted Corinthian pilasters, and in the north aisle is a breadshelf of 1683. Of the 15th century are some tiles and the damaged mural painting of a large kneeling female figure. In the vestry formed from the eastern part of the south chapel is a 17th or 18th century hour glass and a chained library.

HEREFORD *St Peter* SO 512400

The tower at the east end of the south aisle is late 13th century.
The four bay arcades with slender quatrefoil piers, the chancel,
chancel arch, and south chapel were all built in c1300, but the
south arcade, south aisle, west front, and much else besides were
rebuilt by Nicholson in 1880-5. There are several old roofs, that
over the south chapel being low pitched with king-posts and traceried
tie-beams. The 15th century stalls came from St Guthlac's Priory.
The miserichords are carved with roses. The organ case has panels
of c1700, and there are carved royal arms of King William III.
　　Hereford originally had three other medieval churches, but St
Martin and St Olave were destroyed during the siege of 1645, and
St Nicholas was entirely rebuilt in 1842 by Thomas Duckham.

HOLME LACY *St Cuthbert* SO 569347

The church has a long single main body and an equally long south
aisle, both being covered with plaster tunnel vaults of the 1660s.
The east end of the aisle was built first in the late 13th century
with a two bay arcade and Y-traceried windows. The remaining six
bays of the arcade, most of the windows, the south porch, and the
lower part of the west tower are all 14th century. The tower was
completed in the 15th century, and the vestry added in the 19th.
　　The late 17th century font has acanthus and cherubs' heads.
There are 15th century stalls with various creatures carved on the
miserichords, benches with Jacobean and late 17th century work,
and fragments of old glass in a north window. In the south chapel
are fine alabaster effigies of John Scudamore, d1571, and wife,
and a marble monument with a sarcophagus and putti to Viscount Sligo,
d1716. In the chancel is an early 18th century reclining effigy of
James Scudamore, d1668, and a monument to Jane Scudamore, d1699.

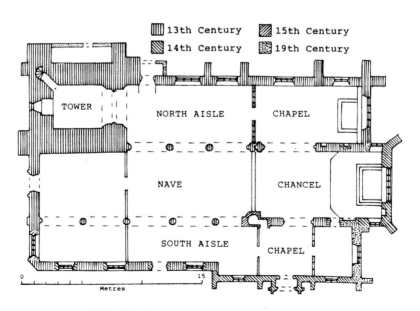

PLAN OF ALL SAINTS' CHURCH, HEREFORD

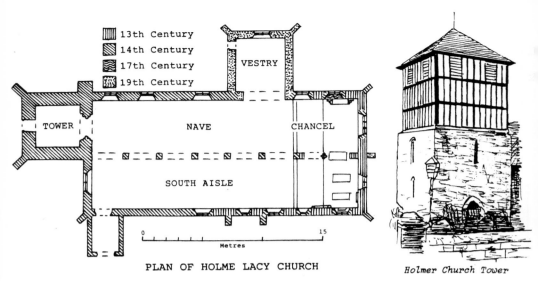

13th Century
14th Century
17th Century
19th Century

VESTRY

TOWER   NAVE   CHANCEL

SOUTH AISLE

0   15
Metres

PLAN OF HOLME LACY CHURCH

Holmer Church Tower

HOLMER *St Bartholomew*   SO 505424

The church comprises a large single chamber of c1190-1220 with a
number of lancet windows, mostly renewed. Above the 19th century
west vestry is a 15th century nave west window. The lower part of
the detached south tower is early 13th century while the timber
framed upper part is 16th century. The church has fine old roofs
with scissor-braced single frames over the nave and hammerbeams and
collar-beams of c1500 with tracery above both in the chancel.

HOPE MANSELL *St Michael*   SO 626197

The nave north wall is Norman with 18th century windows. The east
window and chancel arch are of c1300, but the chancel, with several
lancets, and the walling of a former aisle whose arcade has been
removed so as to widen the nave, are somewhat earlier. The south
doorway is 14th century, and the south porch is 17th century.

HOPE-UNDER-DINMORE *St Mary*   SO 511528

The church was entirely rebuilt by Kempson in 1879 and 1896 but it
contains a 13th century font with Christ and various saints set
under cinquefoiled arches, an incised slab to Humfry Conyngsby,
d1559, and his wife, and a monument of c1760 to Earl Conyngsby and
his wife and an infant son who choked to death on a cherry in 1708.

HOW CAPLE *St Andrew and St Mary*   SO 612305

The chancel is 14th century and has a later low-pitched roof with
bosses. The ashlar faced west tower, nave, and south transept are
all of 1693-5. One 14th century window is re-set in the nave and
the other windows are Victorian. The Late Norman font has vegetable
and geometrical motifs. The pulpit is Jacobean and has a tester.
There are two wings of an early 16th century German altarpiece with
painting on both sides, the carved royal arms of William III, and a
screen with twisted columns and twisted arches also of the 1690s.
There are numerous monuments to members of the Gregory family.

40

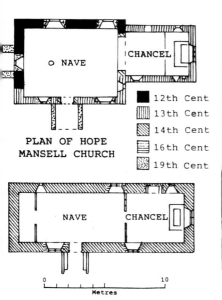

O NAVE

CHANCEL

PLAN OF HOPE
MANSELL CHURCH

■ 12th Cent
▨ 13th Cent
▨ 14th Cent
▤ 16th Cent
▦ 19th Cent

NAVE   CHANCEL

0   10
Metres

PLAN OF HUNTINGTON CHURCH

How Caple Church

HUMBER *St Mary*   SO 536564

The chancel with small lancet windows is of c1200 with a roof of
the 14th century with tie-beams, kingposts, and cusped two way
struts. The nave and the west tower with a broach spire are late
13th century, and the timber south porch is 14th century. The north
chapel and several windows are of 1876-8. The Norman font has a
rope moulding.

HUNTINGTON *St Thomas Beckett*   SO 250534

The thickly walled single chamber is of c1300-20, but also has
three renewed 16th century windows. The timber bell turret and the
massive benches with roughly trefoiled ends are also 16th century.

KENCHESTER *St Michael*   SO 434433

The single chamber has two Norman windows at the east end of the
side walls, doorways of c1200, an east window of c1300, and several
small Victorian windows. A thickening of the west wall carries a
13th century double belfry. The chancel roof is Jacobean and the
font may be an Early Norman remodelling of a Roman stone.

KENDERCHURCH *St Mary*   SO 403284

The nave and chancel masonry is medieval but of features the 1871
restoration has left only the 16th century south doorway, a Norman
font with chevrons, the chancel wagon roof with small bosses, the
Jacobean pulpit, and the top part of the 15th century screen.

KENTCHURCH *St Mary*   SO 419257

The church was entirely rebuilt in 1859. It contains semi-reclining
effigies of John Scudamore, d1616, and his wife, plus ten children.

41

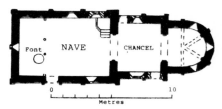

PLAN OF KILPECK CHURCH

Kilpeck church: The south doorway

Kingsland Church

KILPECK *St Mary and St David* SO 445305

The NE corner of the nave, with long and short work, is thought to be Saxon, the chancel has windows and a doorway of c1300, and the bellcote is of 1864. Otherwise this is an unaltered splendid Norman church of c1140-50 comprising a nave, square chancel, and an apse. The church may owe its unusually fine sculptured detailing to the presence from 1134 onwards of a small cell of Benedictine Gloucester Abbey. All round the exterior are pilaster buttresses, some of which clasp the corners, and there is a corbel table. The many motifs carved on the corbels include The Lamb and Cross, two wrestlers, a sheila-na-gig, and a dog and rabbit (all these are upon the apse). The south doorway has one order of colonettes carved with figures, thin trails and beasts' heads, a tympanum with a Tree of Life, and arches with beakheads and linked medallions with dragons and birds. The chancel arch also has figures set one above the other on the colonettes, and chevrons. Further chevrons appear on the ribs of the vault over the apse and on the arches of the nook-shafted apse windows. The stoup with four animal heads and two hands gripping two heads, and the large plain font are also 12th century work.

KIMBOLTON *St James* SO 526616

The chancel is Norman and has two original small windows. Some of the nave masonry may also be Norman, but otherwise the nave, west tower, and south transept are all 13th century. Several windows, and the transept and tower arches were renewed in the 19th century, and the porch then added. The tower has belfry openings with plate tracery and is covered with a tall shingled broach spire. The stall backs with linenfold panels are early 16th century.

42

KING'S CAPLE *St John The Baptist*   SO 559289

The earliest feature is the late 13th century window and recess on
the south side of the large nave. The lower parts of the tower and
several windows in the nave and chancel are 14th century. The upper
part of the tower with a recessed spire, several other windows, and
the south porch and Aramstone chapel on the north side, both with
octopartite rib-vaults, are 15th century. The pulpit and tester,
the front of the stalls, the nave seating, and the box pews in the
chapel are all 17th century, and the west gallery is 18th century.
There are fragments of 15th century glass in the north chapel.

KINGSLAND *St Michael*   SO 447614

The west tower, long aisled nave with five bay arcades, chancel and
north vestry, and the notable north porch with a tiny chapel east
of it, with a tomb recess between it and the aisle, are all work of
c1300-50. The porch entrance is shaped like half of an octagon and
cusped. The nave roof has tie-beams, king-posts, and four-way struts,
and the chancel has a low painted ceiling. The only later portions
are the 15th century tower top and timber south porch, and the 16th
century upper storey of the vestry.

KING'S PYON *St Mary*   SO 438507

Part of the nave north wall is Early Norman. The south doorway with
trumpet capitals on the shafts and the keeled chancel arch responds
are of c1180-1200, when the church was rebuilt and lengthened. The
priest's doorway and south transept are late 13th century. The tomb
recess in the latter is early 14th century and contains late 14th
century effigies of a knight and lady. The west tower and vestry
are also 14th century. The north transept and the organ space are
of 1872. Each has an older window re-set in it.

KINGSTONE *St Michael*   SO 424357

The eastern part of the nave and south doorway are Norman. A north
aisle with a three bay arcade was added in c1200-10, and in 1220-40
the chancel was rebuilt and a two bay north chapel was added to it.
In c1300 the aisle was widened and a tower built west of it, and
then in c1330 the nave was given an ashlar faced extension ending
flush with the tower. There are lancets in the chapel and a late
13th century window in the nave, but the other windows are mostly
of c1330-40. There is a plain Norman font and a dug-out chest.

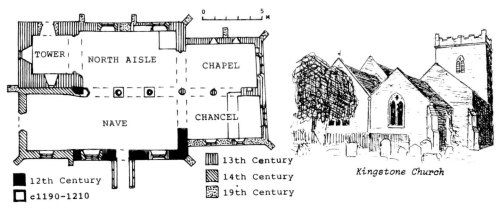

Kingstone Church

PLAN OF KINGSTONE CHURCH   43

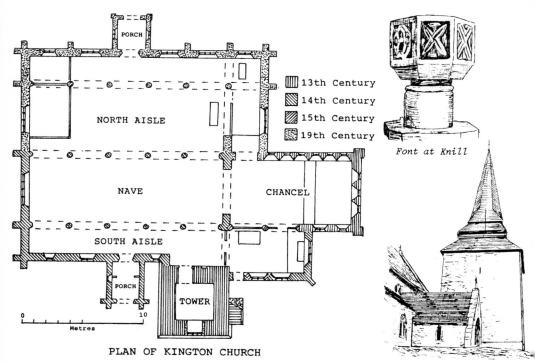

▥	13th Century
▨	14th Century
▧	15th Century
▒	19th Century

NORTH AISLE

NAVE

CHANCEL

SOUTH AISLE

PORCH

TOWER

0   10
Metres

PLAN OF KINGTON CHURCH

Font at Knill

Kington Church Tower

KINGTON *St Mary*   SO 292567

The church lies on a hill west of the town. The oldest part is the
keep-like tower of c1200 in a transeptal position on the south side
which was originally detached. The early 13th century chancel is a
fine structure with three lancets in the east wall and six in the
north wall. The window with Y-tracery on the south side must be of
c1290-5. In c1300-20 the nave was rebuilt and provided with narrow
aisles with five bay arcades, and in c1330-40 a chapel was built
to the south of the chancel. The two bay arcade and one window are
15th century insertions. In 1874 the church was enlarged by greatly
widening the north aisle and adding a narrow outer north aisle with
its own north porch. The font is Norman, with a rope moulding and
chevrons. In the chapel are alabaster effigies on a tomb chest of
Thomas Vaughan, d1469, and his wife, and there is also a substantial
tablet to William Mathews, d1688, in the south aisle.

KINNERSLEY *St James*   SO 346497

The striking feature of the church is the saddleback roofed 14th
century tower projecting west beyond the north aisle. The nave west
wall and doorway are Norman. The chancel is of c1300, the aisles
and timber south porch are of c1300-30, and in the 15th century the
four bay south arcade was renewed and a rood stair turret built at
the east end of it. The north vestry is Victorian. The reredos and
stalls have Jacobean panels, and the pulpit has Flemish allegorical
figures of c1530. In the chancel is a brass to the priest William
Leviot, d1421, and above are kneeling figures of Francis Smallman,
d1635, and wife, with a baldacchino held by cherubs with trumpets.

44

KINSHAM *All Saints*   SO 364649

The renewed windows suggest a date of c1280-1300 for the single
chamber, although there is one possibly older window on the south.
There are fragments of old glass in the east window, some elementary
18th century woodwork, and a tablet to Thomas Harley, d1738.

KNILL *St Michael*   SO 291604

The nave and chancel masonry is Norman, with one original north
window in the chancel. The short west tower and the south doorway
are 13th century, and the octagonal font with knots, crosses, etc
in framed panels is probably of c1200. The rest is all Victorian.

LAYSTERS *St Andrew*   SO 568633

The nave has a Norman south doorway with a roll moulded shouldered
lintel and tympanum, and a blocked original north window. The chancel
is 13th or 14th century, the west tower is early 13th century, and
the nave roof with arched braces going up to collar-beams is 14th
century. All the windows are Victorian.

LEA *St John The Baptist*   SO 658217

The wide north aisle and the chancel were rebuilt by the Victorians.
The aisle west window, one south window, and the spire and tower
top are 14th century. The tower base is late 13th century, and the
three bay north arcade, the north chapel, and the east window are
of the time of the rebuilding of 1418. There are portions of an old
screen, and a large chest dug-out from a trunk, but far more notable
is the font, which is an Italian stoup of c1180-1230 given to Lea
church in 1907. The bowl has a frieze of foliage with human figures
and animals, and stands on a shaft carried by an elephant.

LEDBURY *St Michael*   SO 713377

This is the largest purely parochial church in Herefordshire. From
a large Norman church as long as the present building there remain
the pier bases of a north arcade and the chancel with two windows,
parts of others, clasping corner buttresses, and two bay arcades
for side chapels. In c1200 the nave arcades were renewed and the
west doorway with chevrons and keeled shafts was built. The large
detached tower to the north is early 13th century but the recessed
spire and upper parts were rebuilt in 1727 by Nathaniel Wilkinson.

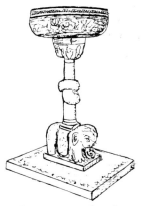

Font at Lea Church

Kinnersley Church

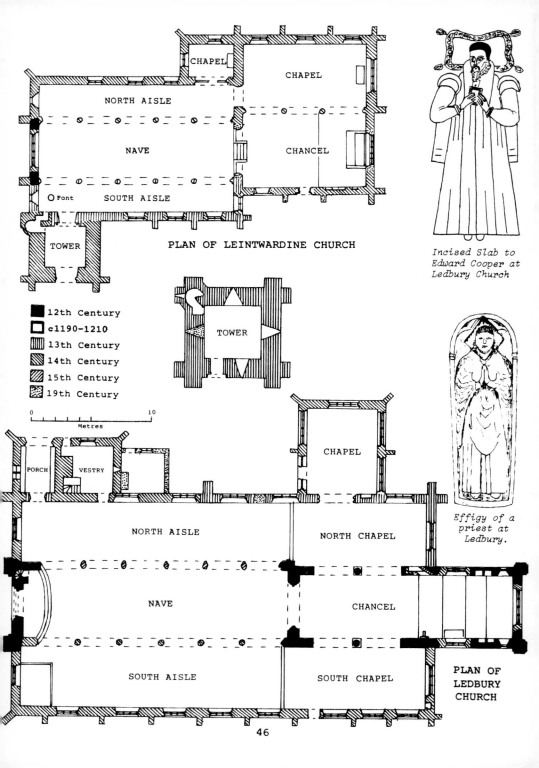

CHAPEL

CHAPEL

NORTH AISLE

NAVE

CHANCEL

O Font SOUTH AISLE

TOWER

PLAN OF LEINTWARDINE CHURCH

Incised Slab to Edward Cooper at Ledbury Church

■ 12th Century
□ c1190-1210
▨ 13th Century
▨ 14th Century
▨ 15th Century
▨ 19th Century

0 ————————— 10
Metres

TOWER

CHAPEL

PORCH VESTRY

NORTH AISLE

NORTH CHAPEL

Effigy of a priest at Ledbury.

NAVE

CHANCEL

SOUTH AISLE

SOUTH CHAPEL

PLAN OF LEDBURY CHURCH

46

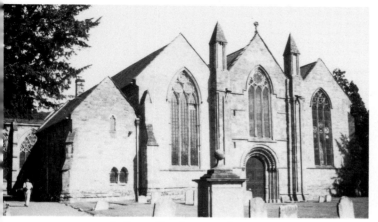

Ledbury Church: west front   *Ledbury: north chapel*

Most of the exterior of the church dates from c1280-1340, when the aisles and chapels were widened, the north aisle being treated first. The aisles have roofs of this period with arched braces to collar-beams and curved wind-braces. Beyond the north chapel is a large outer chapel with huge four light windows studded with ball--flowers. The arcade piers were again renewed but the arches still survive from c1200-10. The two storey NW porch and the vestry east of it are late 14th century.

The stalls are 16th century. Fragments of 13th and 15th century glass appear in several windows. In the chancel are demi-figures of Thomas Thornton, Master of St Katherine's Hospital, d1629, and John Hoskins, rector, d1631, plus kneeling figures of Edward Skinner d1631, and his wife. There are brasses to William Calwe, a kneeling early 15th century priest, Thomas Capel, d1490, and John Hayward, d1614, plus an incised slab to Edward Cooper, d1596. In the south chapel is a bust and trophy to Captain Samuel Skynner, d1725. In the north chapel is a fine but damaged female effigy of c1360, and a late 13th century effigy of a priest is in the outer north chapel.

LEINTHALL EARLS *St Andrew*   SO 443679

The single chamber has a Norman west doorway and windows near the east end, an east window of c1800, other later windows, a timber framed west gable, and an old tie-beam roof with queen-posts.

LEINTHALL STARKES *St Mary Magdalene*   SO 442700

The doorways and three windows of the single chamber are Norman. On the south side are late 13th and 15th century windows. The double bellcote is 17th century, and there is an old roof.

LEINTWARDINE *St Mary Magdalene*   SO 404741

The nave west wall and doorway and the re-set priest's doorway are of c1190-1200. The five bay south arcade and aisle are late 13th century, and the north aisle, the wide chancel, the north chapel, the transeptal chapel west of the latter, and the lofty SW tower with a porch below it, are all 14th century. In the 15th century the north windows were given new tracery, and a clerestory and new low-pitched roof with many bosses built over the nave. The chancel arch and south windows were renewed in the 19th century. On either side of the main east window are remains of a late medieval reredos and there are stalls probably brought here from Wigmore Abbey.

47

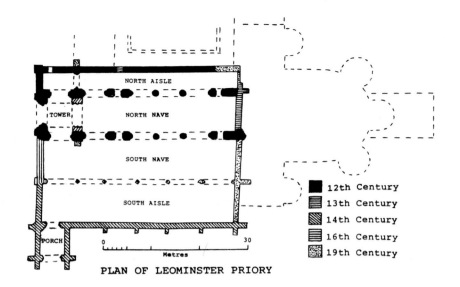

NORTH AISLE

NORTH NAVE

TOWER

SOUTH NAVE

SOUTH AISLE

PORCH

0   30
Metres

■ 12th Century

≣ 13th Century

▨ 14th Century

≣ 16th Century

▨ 19th Century

PLAN OF LEOMINSTER PRIORY

LEOMINSTER *St Peter and St Paul*   SO 498598

A nunnery existing at Leominster in the 9th century was dissolved
in 1046. In 1123 a priory dependent on Reading abbey was founded
for Benedictine monks. The eastern parts of the church must have
been complete by 1130, when a nave altar was consecrated. Composed
of transepts with east apses, and a chancel with an ambulatory with
radiating chapels, these parts were destroyed at the Dissolution.
Little remains also of the monastic buildings north of the church.
The nave still remains and has important work of c1130-50. It seems
the arcades originally had arches alternating with solid sections
of walling, a layout suggesting domes may have been intended, but
before long this scheme was abandoned and part of the layout was
replaced by three adjacent arches on round piers. There is a fine
Norman west doorway and a west tower may have existed, although the
present tower is 15th century. The nave survived because its south
aisle was used by the parish. The aisle was widened in the 13th
century, given a huge new west window in the 15th century, and was
doubled in size by the addition in c1310 of a wide aisle with large
four light windows adorned with ballflowers. The arcade between
the two spaces is of 1872, replacing Tuscan pillars inserted after
a fire of 1699 which destroyed the medieval furnishings. There are
some 14th century tiles in the parochial nave, a wallpainting of a
Wheel of Life of c1275 on the north wall of the monastic nave, and
an old ducking stool in the north aisle.
    The Forbury Chapel, a three bay building of 1282 in the town,
is now an office, having previously been a court house and school.

LETTON *St John The Baptist*   SO 335464

The nave has Early Norman herringbone masonry on the north side.
Of c1180-1200 is the rest of the nave with a south doorway with a
lintel with rosettes and chevrons on the jambs, and a west doorway
with a tufa frieze and tympanum. The chancel is of c1300 and the
south transept with a tomb recess with ballflowers, and the north
tower are 14th century. The south door with fine metalwork is Late
Norman, the plain chancel benches are 17th century, and the pulpit,
tester, and reader's desk are 18th century work from Bristol.

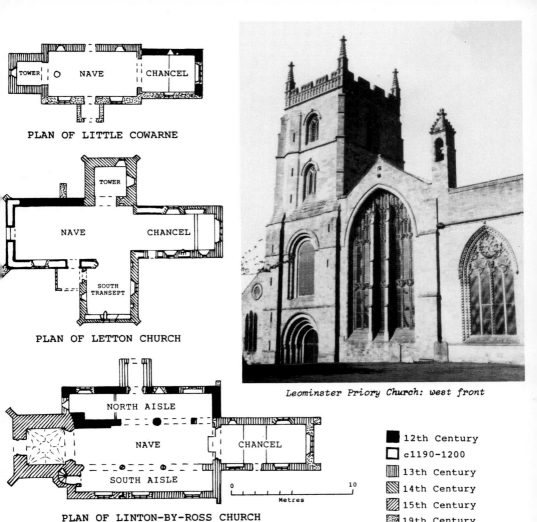

PLAN OF LITTLE COWARNE

PLAN OF LETTON CHURCH

NORTH AISLE

NAVE

SOUTH AISLE

CHANCEL

0   10
Metres

PLAN OF LINTON-BY-ROSS CHURCH

Leominster Priory Church: west front

- 12th Century
- c1190-1200
- 13th Century
- 14th Century
- 15th Century
- 19th Century

LINGEN *St Michael*   SO 366672

The stone parts of the tower and the benches are 16th century. The
rest is of 1891. Inside is a small tablet to John Downes, d1687.

LINTON-BY-ROSS *St Mary*   SO 660254

The masonry and two bay arcade of the north aisle, and one re-set
jamb of a south doorway are Norman. The chancel and south aisle are
13th century. The north wall remains of a Norman west tower which
became part of the nave in the 15th century, when the south aisle
was extended by a new west bay, and a new tower built further west.
The north doorway is 13th century, but the porch is 14th century,
and the chancel east wall is 19th century. There are tablets to
John Elmehurst, d1662, and the Reverend Peter Senhouse, d1760, and
a 13th century coffin lid with an ornate floriated cross upon it.

49

Little Hereford Church

Brass to Thomas Tompkins
at Llandinabo Church

LITTLE BIRCH *St Mary*   SO 505325

A Norman font lies within the church rebuilt in 1869 by W.Chick.

LITTLE COWARNE *Dedication Unknown*   SO 602512

The church was mostly rebuilt in 1869 by Kempson, and the porch is
of 1911. Parts of the chancel, with one window, are Norman, and the
west tower with a saddleback roof, and the nave north wall, with
one original lancet, are 13th century.

LITTLE DEWCHURCH *St David*   SO 529318

Except for the 14th century west tower with a pointed tunnel vault
over the bell chamber, the church was all rebuilt in 1869 by Preedy.

LITTLE HEREFORD *St Mary Magdalene*   SO 554680

A small section of the nave north wall, with one window, is Norman.
Otherwise the nave and the pyramidal roofed west tower are all 13th
century. Of the 14th century are two nave windows, the two tomb
recesses in the south wall, the narrow chancel arch with the rood
stair leading off it, and most of the chancel, including two more
tomb recesses, one with a contemporary female effigy.

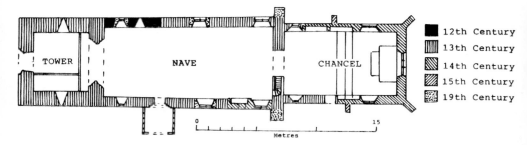

PLAN OF LITTLE HEREFORD CHURCH

LLANCILLO *St Peter*   SO 366256

The small church lies beside the Court. The chancel has a Norman
window and tufa quoins. The east window is 13th century, and two
other windows and the porch are probably 17th century. The chancel
arch and two windows are Victorian. The font is dated 1632 and has
arabesque panels, and there is a 13th century dug-out chest.

LLANDINABO *St Dinabo*   SO 518284

The church was entirely rebuilt in 1881 by A.Lloyd Oswell, leaving
a fine screen of c1520 with a band of dolphins on the cornice, the
partly Jacobean pulpit, and the brass to Thomas Tompkins, a child
who accidentally drowned in 1629. He is shown standing in a pool.

LLANGARRON *St Deinst*   SO 530211

The west tower with a recessed spire, the chancel with a scissor-
braced roof, and the nave south doorway are 14th century. The font,
priest's doorway and a south window are 15th century, other windows
are later, and the north arcade and very wide north aisle are 19th
century. The stone with interlace re-set on the SE buttress is a
relic of the Norman church. The pulpit is Jacobean, and there is
17th century work in the communion rail. There are tablets to Johan
Philpott de Sonke, d1689, Rowland Scudamore, d1697, William Gwllym,
d1698, and Mrs Audley, d1715, and a small 13th century effigy.

LLANROTHAL *St John The Baptist*   SO 471185

The nave now lies derelict and empty. It has a Norman north wall
and a south wall of c1300 with remains of a porch. The late 13th
century chancel has recently been restored to a usable state. It
has a 15th century south window and a Victorian vestry.

LLANVEYNOE *St Peter*   SO 304314

The single chamber is medieval with 19th and 20th century windows.
It has two 11th century panels, one showing a crude Crucifixion.

LLANWARNE *St John The Baptist*   SO 506282

This church now lies in ruins, Christ church to the west having
replaced it in 1864, and taken over the 17th century font. The nave
north wall and the north chapel are 13th century, the south aisle
with a four bay arcade is 14th century, the chancel and west tower
are 15th century, and the south doorway and porch are 17th century.

*Llanwarne
Church
ruins*

LONGTOWN *St Peter*   SO 321291

This church was mostly rebuilt in 1868. It is now being converted
into a house. Both the nave and the chancel, which has one lancet,
are probably 13th century. The east window is 14th century, and the
single framed collar-beam roof over the chancel is dated 1640.

LUCTON *St Peter*   SO 437642

A tablet to John Pierrepont, d1711, lies in the church of 1850.

LUGWARDINE *St Peter*   SO 552410

The 13th century chancel has a row of four lancets in the north
wall. The thick walling of the eastern part of the north aisle is
a relic of the base of a 13th century north tower. Otherwise the
aisle outer walls and the west tower are 15th century. However, the
south aisle west wall looks Norman. It can hardly be a relic of an
aisle of this date which would not be as wide. It could be the old
west wall of the nave re-set, or a 17th century rebuilding. Most of
the windows of the church, the vestries, and the arcades, are of a
restoration by Kempson in 1871-2. There is a brass to Jane Best,
d1622, a semi-reclining effigy of William Reed, d1634, and a demi-
figure of the rector John Best, Jane's husband, d1637.

LYONSHALL *St Michael*   SO 331562

The north arcade has five bays of c1250 and a slightly later west
bay constructed after a Norman west tower had been replaced by a
new rectangular tower beyond. The west wall of the original tower,
with a Norman window, still survives, and the south wall survived
until Bodley added a west bay to the south arcade of c1300 in 1872.
The chancel and north transept, and one south aisle window, are of
c1300, the other windows, vestry, and timber porch being Victorian.
The font is partly 13th century and there is a headless 13th century
effigy of a civilian.

Lyonshall Church   *Madley Church*

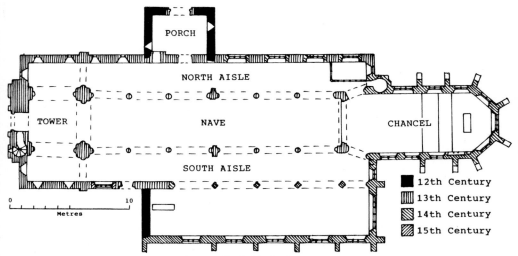

PLAN OF MADLEY CHURCH

12th Century
13th Century
14th Century
15th Century

MADLEY *Nativity of The Virgin*   SO 420388

Madley has a large, attractive, and extremely interesting church.
The north porch is obviously Norman except for the inner and outer
doorways, and was originally the north transept of a cruciform and
aisleless church. Early in the 13th century a west tower was begun,
aisles added with western bays engaging the tower, and the church
greatly lengthened to the east. The arcades have three bays between
the tower and the position of the Norman chancel arch, where there
are wider piers, and then another three bays beyond that. Small
13th century windows remain in the outer walls of the western part
with a doorway on the south side with a 15th century window beside
it. By 1318 a wide new chancel which further lengthened the church
was under construction. It has polygonal ends to both east and
west and is built over a vaulted crypt reached by steps on the south
side. In c1330 the wide outer south aisle or Chilston Chapel was
begun. This has an arcade of five bays and uses the west wall of
the former Norman south transept as its west wall. There are abaci
with ballflowers on the piers and windows with reticulated tracery
which have counterparts inserted in the north aisle east of the
porch. Although now quite light inside, the church would have been
dark when it still had all its medieval glass of which now only a
few fragments remain in the east window and the aisle side windows.
    The large font under the tower is probably Norman. The parclose
screen in the north aisle is 17th century with older parts. There
are stalls with miserichords in the chancel. The west door and the
tower staircase door have 13th century ironwork. Above the chancel
arch are traces of a wall painting. On a tomb chest in the chapel
are recumbent effigies of Richard Willison, d1575, and his wife,
and in the chancel are kneeling figures of Peter Garnons, d1626,
and his wife. In the chapel is a 17th or 18th century reredos.

MANSELL GAMAGE *St Giles*   SO 394445

The south doorway is of c1200 and is covered by a late medieval
timber porch with cusped and traceried bargeboards. Several windows
and the south transept are of c1300, but the north transept, east
window, and several other features are of 1877, while the west tower
is of 1824. The church is now converted into a private house.

Marden Church: The chancel

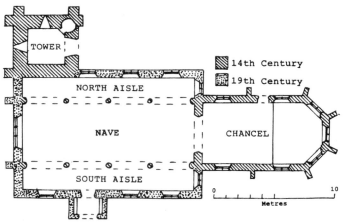

TOWER

NORTH AISLE

NAVE

CHANCEL

SOUTH AISLE

⬚ 14th Century

⬚ 19th Century

0   10

Metres

PLAN OF MARDEN CHURCH

Marden: tower

MANSELL LACY *St Michael*   SO 426456

The blocked north doorway shows that the nave is Norman. The south
aisle with a three bay arcade and the chancel are 13th century, and
the west tower, south porch, and the whole east wall are of the
14th century. One of the original chancel windows is re-set in the
19th century vestry. In the chancel are tablets of 1676 and 1691.

MARDEN *St Mary*   SO 512471

The four bay arcades and the font date from c1280-1300. The aisle
outer walls were rebuilt in 1856 but the south doorway is partly
original. More memorable are the 14th century parts, the tower set
to the north of the west end of the north aisle, with a recessed
spire and its own external doorway, and a chancel with an apse.

MATHON *St John The Baptist* SO 734458

Sections of herringbone masonry and two doorways with plain tympana
only decorated with rope mouldings remain of the small Early Norman
nave and apse. In the late 12th century the building was extended
at both ends to form a long single chamber and the east windows and
priest's doorway are of that period. A north window is 13th century,
and a south one is of c1300, whilst the others are Victorian. The
west tower, timber south porch, and the nave roof with tie-beams
and collar beams are all probably late 14th century. There are two
effigies on a tomb chest of Jane Walweyn, d1617, and her husband.

MICHAELCHURCH *St Michael* SO 522256

The church is said to have been founded in 1056 by Bishop Herwald
of Llandaff but the earliest features of the existing single chamber
are the pair of east windows and north doorway of c1200. Several
other windows are of the same period or slightly later, the south
doorway may be of c1300, and there is one 15th century south window.
The Norman font has a knot frieze, saltire crosses, and interlaced
arches. The frame of the screen is old, and there is 13th century
feigned ashlaring painted on the walls. In the north wall is an
inscribed Roman altar partly cut back to form a rough capital.

MICHAELCHURCH ESCLEY *St Michael* SO 307342

The nave is probably Norman. It and the 16th century chancel form a
single chamber. One window is 15th century, three are 17th, and the
south doorway is 18th century, although the porch is 16th century.
The wagon roof with small bosses is late medieval. The west tower
and three of the chancel windows are Victorian. On the north wall
is a mural painting of Christ and the tools of the trades.

MIDDLETON-ON-THE-HILL *St Mary* SO 541646

The 13th century west tower is large compared with the Norman nave
and chancel which have pilaster buttresses and several original
windows and doorways with chevrons on the arches. Three windows are
late 13th century and the east window of c1300 is from Pudleston
church. The font is also Norman, and has a chevron band.

MOCCAS *St Michael* SO 357434

Except for the bellcote, and the four windows and timber porch of
the 14th century, this is an all-Norman church comprising a nave,
square chancel, and an apse which preserves its original windows.
The church is built of tufa, but the nave doorways are sandstone.
They have one order of shafts, and tympana, now very worn. That on
the south was a Tree of Life, whilst on the north was a beast and
scrolls. The 14th century windows have the remains of contemporary
glass, and of the same period is the effigy of a cross-legged knight.

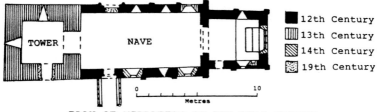

PLAN OF MIDDLETON-ON-THE-HILL CHURCH

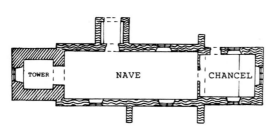

PLAN OF MONNINGTON-ON-WYE CHURCH

Monnington Church

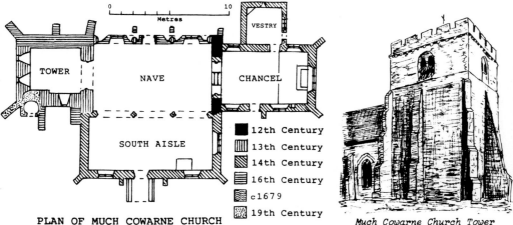

PLAN OF MUCH COWARNE CHURCH

12th Century
13th Century
14th Century
16th Century
c1679
19th Century

Much Cowarne Church Tower

MONKLAND *All Saints*   SO 460577

The nave has two Norman windows on each side. Two north windows and
the west tower are late 13th century, and two south windows and the
doorway are 14th century. Street rebuilt the chancel in 1866.

MONNINGTON-ON-WYE *St Mary*   SO 374434

The 15th century west tower has large battlements with cruciform
arrow slits. The rest of the church, comprising nave, chancel, and
a north porch, was rebuilt for Uvedale Tomkyns in 1679, and the
screen, communion rail, pulpit, font, panelling, benches, and the
finely carved arms of Charles II are all of that date. There is a
ledger stone to Uvedale Tomkyns and a bust of Robert Perrot, d1667.

MORDIFORD *Holy Rood*   SO 571375

The nave has a Norman south doorway with one order of shafts and
chevrons on the arch, and re-set in the vestry is a doorway of c1200.
A central tower and a new chancel were added in the 13th century.
A new tower projecting from the west end of the nave south wall was
built in c1811, and the upper parts of the older tower were then
removed. The north aisle, the small chapel opening off the nave,
and most of the windows are of the late 19th century.

MORETON JEFFRIES *Dedication Unknown*   SO 604485

The single chamber has a 14th century doorway, a chancel roof with beams and raking struts, and a 17th century pulpit and tester.

MORETON-ON-LUGG *St Andrew*   SO 505456

The rebuilding of 1867 by W.H. Knight left only a Norman window in the chancel, the late medieval three bay arcade and aisle eastern window, the single framed collar-beam roof in the nave, and the screen with a band of running vine on the cornice, and cresting.

MUCH COWARNE *St Mary*   SO 618472

A late Norman doorway is re-set in the central arch of the blocked three bay arcade of a 13th century north aisle demolished in the 16th century. The west tower is probably early 13th century, but one window looks Norman, the north wall and buttresses are of the 16th century, and a new stair turret was provided after the spire was destroyed by lightning in 1840. The wide south aisle and three bay arcade, plus the chancel, and possibly also the vestry, are of c1300, and the east window is late 14th century. In the aisle is a damaged late 13th century effigy of a knight, and a tomb chest with recumbent effigies of Edmund Fox, d1617, and his wife. On the sides are ten kneeling children and three babies in a cradle. An effigy of Sybil Reed, d1624, lies in the chancel.

MUCH DEWCHURCH *St David*   SO 483311

The nave and chancel are both Norman. Three original windows still remain partially or wholly, plus the plain chancel arch and south doorway with a tympanum. The west tower is 13th century. There are several south windows of c1280-1320, and the east window is late 14th century. The pyramidal roof of the tower, the north aisle and its two bay arcade, and the vestry are all Victorian. The porch is 14th century. The Norman font has arcading, small heads and flowers, and the pulpit is Jacobean. Part of a foliated 13th century coffin lid forms a shaft by the altar. There are recumbent effigies of c1570 to John and Walter Pye, kneeling figures of Walter Pye, d1625, and his wife, and a tablet to John Symons, d1763.

Monnington Church Porch

*Much
Dewchurch
Church*

MUCH MARCLE

St Bartholomew SO 657327

Much Marcle Church

Although the south doorway and the aisle outer walls may be slightly later, the four bay arcades are both of c1230-40, and there is a clerestory of single lancets above. Several windows are of c1300, having Y-tracery, and at that time the chancel was extended and provided with a chapel with a two bay arcade. The chancel was given a new classical style priest's doorway in the 18th century, and in the 19th the chapel north wall was rebuilt, and a vestry added alongside. There are indications of older arches on either side of the 15th century central tower, so an older tower and transepts may once have existed.

The communion rail is late 17th century, and there is a heraldic panel of 1628 in the north chapel east window. The recess in the north wall of the chancel contains a fine effigy of Blanche Mortimer, Lady Grandison, d1347. In the south aisle is an oak effigy of a man of c1370, and in the north chapel is a tomb chest with two effigies of c1400, and a black and white marble tomb chest with effigies of Sir John Kyrle, d1650, and his wife.

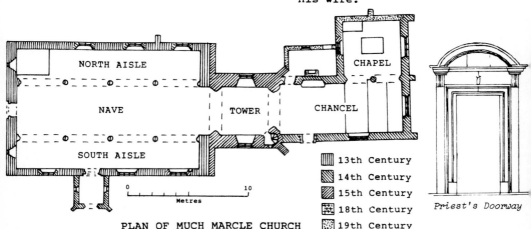

NORTH AISLE

NAVE

SOUTH AISLE

TOWER

CHAPEL

CHANCEL

0 ⊢⊢⊢⊢⊢⊢⊢⊢⊢⊢ 10
Metres

▥	13th Century
▨	14th Century
▧	15th Century
▦	18th Century
▨	19th Century

Priest's Doorway

PLAN OF MUCH MARCLE CHURCH

MUNSLEY *St Bartholomew*   SO 663410

The nave and chancel are both Early Norman with several original
windows, a plain chancel arch, and herringbone masonry in the east
wall. Other windows and the nave doorways are 14th century. The
slab with an illegible inscription in the south wall may be Saxon.

NEWTON *St John The Baptist*   SO 347329

The church was rebuilt in 1842 but contains a pulpit of c1660.

NORTON CANON *St Nicholas*   SO 382478

The NW tower with clasping buttresses and a pyramidal roof is 13th
century. The nave, chancel, and shallow transepts are of brick and
were under construction in 1718. Re-set in them are the windows of
c1300 from the medieval church, and two contain contemporary glass
of the grisaille type. The communion rail, pulpit, and reredos all
incorporate early 17th century material.

OCLE PYCHARD *St James*   SO 596463

The eastern part of the nave and the south doorway are perhaps 13th
century, while the western third of the nave, the chancel, and the
NE vestry are all 14th century. The west wall has a doorway flanked
by buttresses both inside and outside which support a tiny tower. The
copper covered broach spire on the tower is fairly recent.

ORCOP *St Mary*   SO 474263

The west tower has a weatherboarded timber upper storey with heavy
timbers supporting it inside. The narrow north aisle and its three
bay arcade is early 13th century and there is a late 13th century
window in the chancel, and the south doorway is 14th century. Other
windows, and the polygonal vestry are of 1860, by T.Nicholson. The
nave has a fine old wagon roof. In the chancel is the top part of
a scalloped Norman pillar piscina.

ORLETON *St George*   SO 495673

The nave is Norman and has an original west window, now blocked by
the 13th century tower. The tower doorway of c1200 is probably re-
set. The early 13th century chancel has several lancet windows, and
the chancel arch and the tie-beam roof with king-posts and queen-
posts may be 14th century. The vestry is Victorian. The Late Norman
font has nine apostles standing under arches. There are two 13th
century dug-out chests, some fragments of 14th century glass in
the nave windows, and a fine mid-17th century pulpit.

Orcop Church

PLAN OF MUNSLEY CHURCH

NAVE

0   10
Metres

■ 12th Century
▨ 14th Century
▧ 19th Century

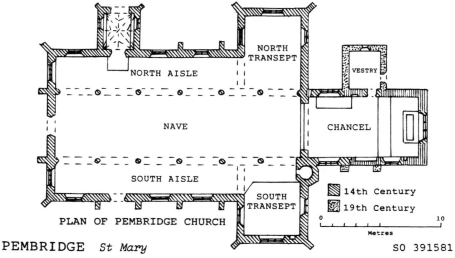

NORTH TRANSEPT

NORTH AISLE

VESTRY

NAVE

CHANCEL

SOUTH AISLE

SOUTH TRANSEPT

PLAN OF PEMBRIDGE CHURCH

14th Century

19th Century

0   10

Metres

PEMBRIDGE *St Mary*

SO 391581

The chancel masonry is 13th century and has traces of arches which opened into former chapels, but the windows, and the whole of the rest of the church, are of c1320-60. There are transepts and aisles with six bay arcades above which are circular and cinquefoiled clerestory windows, a vaulted north porch, and rood stair turret covered with a pinnacle beside the chancel arch. The single framed nave roof is original but much restored. Instead of a tower there is an unusual detached bellhouse which is a pyramidal roofed wooden structure surrounded by a low stone-walled ambulatory.

The font is 13th century, and the north door and the fragments of old glass in the aisle west windows are 14th century. The pulpit, reader's desk, lectern, and communion rail are all Jacobean. On tomb chests are effigies of an early 14th century civilian and lady, and a later 14th century knight and lady. In the chancel are tablets to the wives of William and Essex Sherborne, d1660, and 1668, and there are larger tablets to William Sherborne, d1671, and Thomas Trafford, d1685. All of them have pairs of putti.

Pembridge Church

Pembridge: 14th century tombs in the chancel

PENCOYD *St Dennis*   SO 516266

The nave and west tower are 14th century, and have several windows
of that period. The chancel was entirely rebuilt in 1877-8.

PETERCHURCH *St Peter*   SO 345385

This large and little altered Norman church has four compartments,
a nave, former or intended central tower, chancel, and east apse.
The south doorway, with an original door, and the arches between
the compartments are decorated with chevrons. The apse has pilaster
buttresses on the outside, and the tub-shaped font has rope mouldings
and a nutmeg frieze. Later additions are the 13th century window in
the chancel, a 14th century window in the nave, two 15th century
windows in the central body, and the west tower begun in c1280 and
completed in the 14th century with a lofty recessed spire.

PETERSTOW *St Peter*   SO 564249

The nave has one Norman north window, and one 13th century lancet.
The doorway, other windows, scissor braced roof, and the chancel
are 14th century, and the thin west tower and spire are of the 15th
century. The pulpit is Jacobean, and has blank arches.

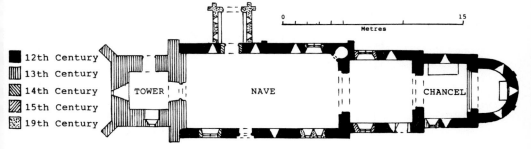

PLAN OF PETERCHURCH CHURCH

PIPE-AND-LYDE *St Peter*

G.Kempson rebuilt the nave in 1874, leaving only the 13th century and Late Norman north and south doorways. He also added a broach spire to the 13th century west tower. The chancel is of c1300 and has a splendid roof with collars on arched braces with a trefoiled opening above. The original rood beam, with foliage, also survives.

PIXLEY *St Andrew*

The small single chamber has a tie-beam roof and old posts which now support a Victorian bell-turret. There are original lancets in the east wall, and a later 13th century window, plus others of the 16th or 17th centuries, in the south wall. The screen is old and the south doorway has a large 13th century hinge.

PRESTON-ON-WYE *St Lawrence*

The church was heavily restored by T.Nicholson in 1883 but has a Late Norman doorway with chevrons on the arch and trumpet scallop capitals to the colonettes. Also Norman are one north window and the north doorway, with a later head. The priest's doorway is of c1300, and the west tower and north transept are 14th century. The pulpit and the bench ends with leaf decoration are Jacobean.

PRESTON WYNNE *Holy Trinity*

The church lies in a field. It was built in 1730 but the nave and chancel were both given new gothic features in the 19th century.

PUDLESTON *St Peter*

The nave west wall has a Norman window now looking into the tower of c1300 upon which is a later medieval spire. Otherwise, the nave was rebuilt in 1813, and given aisles in 1851. The chancel is 13th century, but has an east window and vestries of the 1850s.

Richard's Castle Church: west front

*Coffin Lid,
Richard's Castle*

Richard's Castle Church: Chancel and tower

PUTLEY   *Dedication Unknown*   SO 646376

The nave has two doorways and two windows of the 14th century. The
chancel and long vestry are of 1875. The pulpit and screen contain
re-used Jacobean work. Much of the churchyard cross is preserved.

RICHARDS CASTLE   *St Bartholomew*   SO 484703

The church lies on a hill beside the castle, and in order to help
rather than hinder defence of the latter has a detached tower of
c1300 to the east, overlooking the approach. The nave is Norman and
has two original windows in the north wall. The chancel masonry is
probably of c1190-1200, but the windows are 14th century, as are
the south aisle with a three bay arcade, and the north transept
with a two bay arcade. The pier of the latter and the chancel arch
responds have castellated capitals with fleurons. The west window
and porch are 15th century, and the unusual tracery of the transept
end window may be 17th century. There was once a medieval vestry.
Several windows contain fragments of old glass, and there are box
pews once dated 1688, and a 13th century coffin lid with a cross.

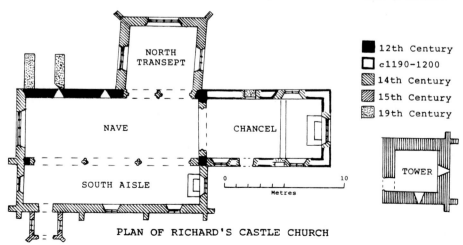

	12th Century
	c1190-1200
	14th Century
	15th Century
	19th Century

PLAN OF RICHARD'S CASTLE CHURCH

63

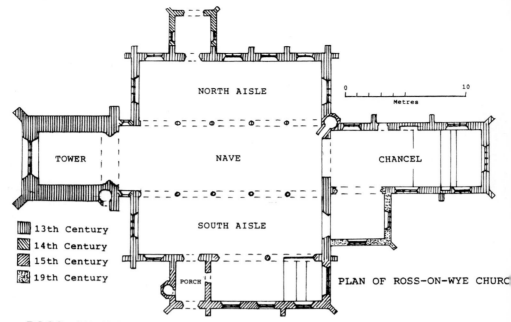

NORTH AISLE

TOWER   NAVE   CHANCEL

0   10
Metres

SOUTH AISLE

	13th Century
	14th Century
	15th Century
	19th Century

PORCH

PLAN OF ROSS-ON-WYE CHURCH

ROSS-ON-WYE *St Mary*   SO 598241

Ross has one of the largest churches in Herefordshire. The chancel and the wide aisles are of c1280-1300, and the west tower and north porch are early 14th century. Later medieval additions are the east end of the chancel, the south porch, and the Markey chapel east of the latter. The south and north arcades are of c1200 and c1220-40 respectively. Their lower parts date from when they were raised in 1743 to make the interior appear more spacious.

The font, pulpit and communion rail are all late 17th century. Four 15th century stained glass figures in the east window have come from the mansion of the Bishops of Hereford at Stretton Sugwas. On an alabaster tomb chest are fine effigies of William Rudhall, d1530, Attorney General to Henry VIII, and his wife. There are tablets to William Rudhall, d1609, Nathaniel Hill, d1632, Elizabeth Markey, d1681, George Rudhall, d1729, a tomb chest with alabaster effigies of John Rudhall, d1636, and his wife, and a standing figure of Col. William Rudhall, d1651.

ROTHERWAS *Dedication Unknown*   SO 536384

The date 1589 on one of the tie-beams of the fine roof with queen-posts supporting hammerbeams with pendants refers to a rebuilding for Sir Robert Bodenham. One north window is 14th century, and two others are probably early 16th century. The west tower is probably 18th century, and the east end is all Victorian.

ROWLSTONE *St Peter*   SO 374271

Both the nave and chancel have several original Norman windows and the south doorway has birds carved on the capitals of the shafts, a roll moulding, a band of rosettes, and a tympanum depicting Christ in Glory. There are also birds and figures on the capitals of the narrow chancel arch. The east window is 15th century, the tower is ancient but of uncertain date, and the south porch is Victorian.

ST DEVEREUX *St Dubricius*   SO 441312

The tomb recesses and paired lancets date the nave to the late 13th
century, and the west tower may be of the same period. The chancel
is late 14th century. There are ledgerstones to Thomas Goode, d1664,
and Ann Goode, d1668, and fragments of other 17th century monuments.

ST MARGARETS *St Margaret*   SO 354337

The narrow chancel arch, and probably the nave masonry, are Norman.
One south window dates the chancel to c1300. Three domestic type
windows may be 17th century, and the porch may be 19th century.
Much more important are the very finely carved rood screen and loft
of c1520. The loft coving rests on two posts.

ST WEONARDS *St Weonard*   SO 497243

The nave south wall and chancel arch are of c1300, and the chancel
and south vestry are Victorian. The west tower and the north aisle
and chapel are 16th century, although the arches of the four bay
arcade to the aisle may be re-used 13th century material. The porch
is also 16th century and has a stoup with a large face. The chapel
is closed off by original screens. There are fragments of old glass,
a Jacobean pulpit, a 13th century dug-out chest, and an obelisk,
urn, and cherubs' heads in memory of Robert Minors Gouge, d1765.

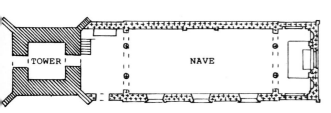

PLAN OF STOKE EDITH CHURCH

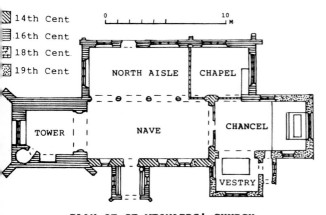

⟋ 14th Cent
≣ 16th Cent
⊞ 18th Cent.
▨ 19th Cent

0   10
M

PLAN OF ST WEONARDS' CHURCH

The tower, Ross on Wye.

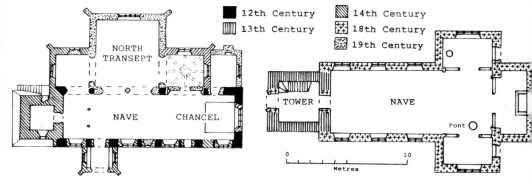

■ 12th Century	▨ 14th Century
▥ 13th Century	▦ 18th Century
	▩ 19th Century

PLAN OF SELLACK CHURCH   PLAN OF SHOBDON CHURCH

SARNESFIELD *St Mary*   SO 375510

The **Norman** nave has a west window now looking into a tower of c1300
in which is re-set another Norman window. The narrow south aisle
with a four bay arcade is of c1190, but the doorway and two of the
windows are of c1300. The chancel and south chapel, with a two bay
arcade between them, are early 14th century. Also 14th century are
the fine tie-beam roof over the nave, the timber south porch, and
the stained glass figures in the south chapel. Outside, west of the
porch, is the tomb of John Abel. He designed many timber buildings
in Herefordshire, and died in 1674, aged 97.

SELLACK *St Tysilio*   SO 566277

The **two eastern** bays of a Norman three bay north arcade and early
14th century aisle were obliterated by the building of a Victorian
north transept. Between the transept and the 19th century vestry is
a vaulted 15th century chapel with a 13th century arch towards the
14th century chancel. Also 14th century are the south porch and the
west tower with a broach spire. The pulpit and tester, the altar
panelling, and the west gallery are Jacobean. The stained glass in
the east window is of 1630, with older fragments. There are tablets
to Helip Fox, d1768, William Powell, d1680, and Thomas Symonds, d1760.

SHOBDON *St John*   SO 401628

Except for the 13th century west tower the whole church was rebuilt
in 1752-6. It has a nave with a shallow chancel bay screened off,
and equally shallow transepts. The south transept accommodated the
Bateman family who paid for the rebuilding, and the north transept
seated their servants. The work is of ashlar, with battlements and
ogival gothick arches. The interior is particularly notable, having
a full set of contemporary matching furnishings painted white with
some light blue. There is also some stained glass of 1753.

On the hillside some distance north of the church and house is
a folly formed from the re-erected chancel arch and doorways of the
original Norman church of c1135, built to serve a small Augustinian
priory later moved to Eye, and then to Wigmore. The doorway tympana
represent the Harrowing of Hell and Christ in Glory, and the jambs
have a profusion of dragons, birds, medallions, lions, interlace,
chevrons, and human figures. The carvings are now very decayed but
luckily drawings and reproductions of them were made before they
were allowed to become eroded away.

Shobdon Arches

Stoke Edith Church

SOLLERS HOPE *St Michael*   SO 613331

The nave, chancel, and porch are 14th century, but the windows are mostly 15th century and have some fragments of old glass. Two posts inside the nave carry a timber belfry and spire. There is an early incised slab of c1225 depicting a knight, and a Jacobean pulpit.

STANFORD BISHOP *St James*   SO 682516

The nave has two doorways and two windows of c1190; another window is re-set in the 14th century chancel. The west tower is early 13th century and there is a rebuilt 14th century porch. The south door is original, and there is a Jacobean pulpit and a medieval chair.

STAUNTON-ON-WYE *St Mary*   SO 376448

The nave has Late Norman doorways, a 13th century lancet, and 14th century windows. The pyramidal roofed west tower is of c1300, and the 18th century chancel has Victorian windows. Only the crude two bay arcade remains of a former transeptal north chapel. Under the tower are Jacobean panels, medallions of c1540, and the 17th century communion rail. Outside is a defaced 14th century female effigy.

STOKE EDITH *St Mary*   SO 604407

The 14th century west tower has a recessed needle spire. The Foleys of Stoke Edith Park had the church itself rebuilt in brick in 1740. There are five bays with huge Tuscan columns dividing off the ends. Each end of the south wall has a doorway, but one is a dummy built for the sake of symmetry. Contemporary with the church are the font, communion rails, pews, and three decker pulpit. An alabaster effigy depicts a late 15th century lady with a butterfly head-dress, and there is a large monument to Paul Foley, d1699, and two identical tablets to Henry Wolstenholme, d1738, and his wife, d1749.

STOKE LACY *St Peter and St Paul*   SO 621494

The rebuilding of 1863 by Kempson left only the Norman chancel arch
and the low screen with a running leaf frieze on the cornice.

STRETFORD *St Peter*   SO 443558

In the 13th century the Norman church, of which one north window
remains, was given a new chancel and a wide south aisle which now
serves as the nave. The east and west windows are 14th century but
the west wall itself is a Victorian rebuild. The original separate
roofs were replaced in c1530 by a new single span roof over the
whole width. It has one tie-beam, arched braces to collar-beams,
and four tiers of cusped wind braces. The centrally placed belfry
turret and the south porch may be of the same period. There is a
Norman font and a Jacobean pulpit. the recess in the north wall has
effigies of two couples of the Delabere family of c1320 and c1350.

STRETTON GRANDISON *St Lawrence*   SO 633441

The roll-moulded priest's doorway is a re-set piece of c1200. The
nave, chancel, west tower, and porch are otherwise all of c1300-50.
A contemporary wall painting of a lady appears above the doorway.
The Easter Sepulchre in the chancel has been cut through for access
to a Victorian vestry. The font and pulpit are 15th century, and
there is a tablet to Sir Edward Hopton, d1668, and his wife.

STRETTON SUGWAS *St Mary Magdalene*   SO 460420

The new church of 1877-80 incorporates various relics of the old
church. The timber framed upper parts of the tower and several of
the windows are late medieval, there are old tiles in the vestry,
one being dated 1456, and the tower doorway and the south doorway
tympanum which depicts Samson and the Lion are Norman. Also there
is an incised slab depicting Richard Grevelhey and his wife, d1473.

Stretton
Sugwas:
The tower

*Incised
Slab at
Stretton
Sugwas*

PLAN OF SUTTON ST MICHAEL CHURCH

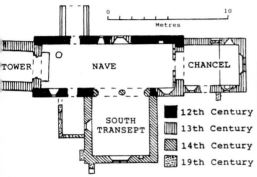

■	12th Century
▥	13th Century
▨	14th Century
▦	19th Century

PLAN OF SUTTON ST NICHOLAS CHURCH

Tarrington Church

SUTTON *St Nicholas*   SO 534454

The chancel and narrow nave are both of c1200, the chancel arch, north doorway, and two windows being of about that date. The west tower is 13th century, the south transept and its two bay arcade are early 14th century, and the chancel has three windows of c1300. The nave and chancel have 14th century piscinas with ballflowers. The timber north porch is 14th century. The screen has linenfold panels of c1520 in the dado, and there is a Jacobean pulpit.

SUTTON *St Michael*   SO 527458

The small nave and chancel are both Norman and have three original windows. The four south windows are of c1300-20. In the west wall is the blocked arch of a former 13th century tower, now replaced by a timber porch. There is a Norman font with four busts of lions against the base and there is also a rare mid-17th century font in the form of a classical urn carried by a demi-figure of an angel holding a book. The tablet to Elizabeth Cotton, d1654, has standing allegorical figures, a pediment, putti, and a corpse in a shroud.

TARRINGTON *St Philip and St James*   SO 618408

Much of the church is Norman and there was originally an apse. The nave doorways with one order of shafts are original, that on the north being re-set in the wall of the aisle added in 1835. Also Norman are two chancel windows, the chancel arch jambs, and the altered tower arch. However the tower itself is 15th century and the chancel has 15th century windows. The nave south wall has been refaced. The font is late medieval and there are fragments of old glass. There is an old coffin lid with a cross and an effigy of a lady of c1340 set in a tomb recess of c1320 with ballflowers.

TEDSTONE DELAMERE   *St James*   SO 696585

The nave has two Norman windows of tufa and a 13th century lancet.
The tiny chancel was rebuilt in 1856-7 by Sir G.G.Scott. The screen
is late medieval, and there is an old hourglass in the porch.

TEDSTONE WAFRE   *St Mary*   SO 677591

Only a fragment of the south wall remains of the Early Norman old
church. The new church of 1873 is being converted into a residence.

THORNBURY   *St Anne*   SO 623597

The Norman nave has an original window beside a shafted doorway
with chevrons on the arch. The massive west tower and the blocked
three bay arcade of a former south aisle are 13th century and the
nave has a north window of c1300. The chancel, vestry, and porch
are of 1865 by Kempson. The Norman tub shaped font has lozenges.

THRUXTON   *St Bartholomew*   SO 437347

The west tower, short chancel, timber south porch, and the nave
with its scissor braced roof are all 14th century. The chancel has
a contemporary Crucifixus in the south window, whilst the eastern
window is late 14th century. The font is inscribed and dated 1677.

TURNASTONE   *St Mary Magdalene*   SO 357364

The Norman nave and the late 13th century chancel form a single
undivided chamber. The nave has four late 13th century windows, and
the chancel east window is probably late 16th century. There is a
fine ceiled roof with bosses, a simple Jacobean pulpit, and an
incised slab to Thomas Aparri, d1522, and his wife, and a tablet to
Mrs Tranter, d1685, with rustic motifs and allegorical figurines.

TYBERTON   *St Mary*   SO 380399

Apart from the Late Norman south doorway, and the windows of 1879,
the brick church and its furnishings are of 1719-21. There are
monuments to William Brydges, d1668, Margaret Brydges, d1671, Anne
Brydges, d1696, Francis Brydges, d1727, and his first wife, d1691,
William Brydges, d1764, and Francis Brydges, d1793.

ULLINGSWICK   *Dedication Unknown*   SO 596500

The Norman nave has two original windows. It was lengthened to the
west in the 13th century and a new chancel built in c1300. The east
window has a 15th century stained glass bust of the Virgin and Child.
There is a recumbent effigy of John Hill, d1591, on a tomb chest,
and a 13th century coffin lid with a floriated cross.

UPPER SAPEY   *St Michael*   SO 684637

The nave has two Norman doorways with two orders of shafts and
chevrons on the arches, and the chancel has a Norman north window.
The nave was lengthened westwards in c1200, and has a window of
that date. Three south windows are of c1300, and there are other
windows, a chancel arch and a west tower of 1859, etc. The original
Norman chancel arch, similar to the doorways, is re-set as the new
tower arch. There are four plain early 16th century benches.

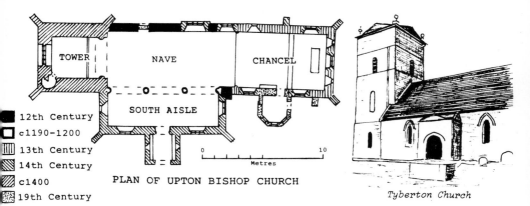

TOWER | NAVE | CHANCEL

SOUTH AISLE

- ■ 12th Century
- □ c1190–1200
- ▥ 13th Century
- ▨ 14th Century
- ▧ c1400
- ▦ 19th Century

0   10
Metres

PLAN OF UPTON BISHOP CHURCH

Tyberton Church

UPTON BISHOP   *St John The Baptist*   SO 651273

The nave has a blocked Norman north doorway. The three bay arcade is of c1180, but the aisle was rebuilt in the 14th century, and the porch then added. The 13th century chancel is the same width as the nave. It had three lancets in the east wall, but the middle one was replaced by a larger window in the 14th century. The west tower is of c1400, the font is 15th century, the pulpit is Jacobean, and there is a 14th century effigy of a civilian under an ogival canopy. On the chancel south wall is part of a Roman tombstone with a figure.

URISHAY   *Dedication Unknown*   SO 323376

Beside Urishay Castle is a Norman chapel with a ruined nave and a recently re-roofed chancel the same width divided by a narrow round chancel arch. The doorways are old, but the windows are 19th century.

VOWCHURCH   *St Bartholomew*   SO 362365

One window, the font, and parts of the nave walls are Norman. The church was reconsecrated in 1348 after being extended into a long single chamber, now divided by a screen of 1613. Although it has some Jacobean decoration, the roof is 14th century work, as are the posts now supporting a bell turret of the 1520s. There are stalls with backs dated 1632, and a communion rail of the 1670s.

Urishay Chapel

PLAN OF VOWCHURCH CHURCH

NAVE   CHANCEL

■ 12th C
▥ 13th C
▨ 14th C
▧ 15th C
▥ 17th C
▦ 19th C

TOWER

PORCH

NORTH AISLE   CHAPEL

NAVE   CHANCEL

PORCH

0 — Metres — 10

Weobley Church Tower

WALFORD-ON-WYE CHURCH

WALFORD-ON-WYE *St Michael*   SO 587204

The church is mostly of various dates within the 13th century and
comprises a nave with a north aisle with a four bay arcade, the
chancel with an arcade of three small arches to a north chapel, and
a north tower projecting beyond the chapel. The chancel south
windows are 14th century, and the east windows, north doorway, font
and south porch are 15th century. The communion rail is of c1700,
and there are tablets to William Adams, d1681, Edmund Yerne, d1707,
John Stratford, d1738, and a group of other Stratfords up to 1709.

WALTERSTONE *St Mary*   SO 340250

The Norman nave has a late medieval doorway, and Victorian windows
and bellcote. One of the two late 14th century chancel windows has
17th century glass. There are slate tablets to the Price family.

WELLINGTON *St Margaret*   SO 497483

The spacious nave, the chancel arch, and the two doorways, one now
re-set in the aisle, are Norman, and of c1180-1200 is the massive
west tower with pilaster buttresses pierced by windows. The chancel
is late 13th century, and the tomb recess within it, and the south
porch are early 14th century. Of the late 14th century are the four
bay north arcade, the north aisle with its fine roof, and the north
transept. There is also a tablet to Sir Herbert Perrot, d1683.

WELSH BICKNOR *St Margaret*   SO 592177

A late 13th century female effigy lies in the church of 1858-9.

Weston-Under-Penyard Church

Welsh Newton Church

WELSH NEWTON *St Mary*   SO 499180

The church is mostly 13th century and forms a single chamber with
a tiny west tower and spire flanked by lancets. It is covered by a
wagon roof with ribs and bosses. The stone seat in the chancel may
be 13th century. Of the 14th century are the very rare stone screen
lighted by a dormer window, and the porch. In the churchyard is the
tomb of John Kemble, a catholic priest executed in August 1679.

WEOBLEY *St Peter and St Paul*   SO 402519

The re-set south doorway with chevrons is all that remains of the
Norman church. The chancel and south aisle are late 13th century,
and shortly before the consecration of three altars in 1325 a north
transept and aisle, and new five bay arcades were provided. Then the
lofty NW tower with a spire connected to corner pinnacles by flying
buttresses was begun. The chancel was lengthened in the late 14th
century, and the north aisle was widened in the 15th century.

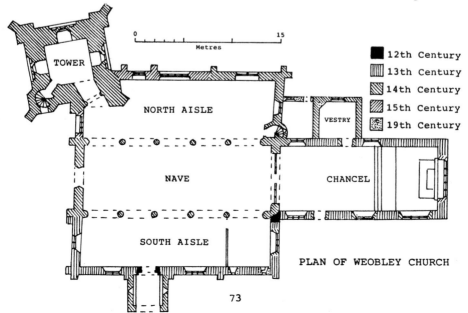

PLAN OF WEOBLEY CHURCH

Weobley Church

Of the 14th century are the font and parts of a stone pulpit. In the north aisle are fragments of an old screen and five 15th century stained glass figures. In the south aisle is a 13th century coffin lid with a fine floriated cross in memory of Hugh Bissop of Norton Canon. The alabaster knight on a tomb chest may be William Devereux, d1430. There are alabaster effigies of Dame Alice Crutwell and John Marbury, d1437, and a statue of Colonel John Birch, d1691.

WESTHIDE *St Bartholomew*   SO 586442

The pyramidal roofed tower is Late Norman, and the wide south aisle with a two bay arcade and a recess with an effigy of a man holding his heart is 14th century. The tower west wall has been rebuilt and the nave north wall and chancel were renewed in 1866-7. An incised slab depicts Richard Monyington, d1524, and his wife and sixteen children, and there is a damaged Elizabethan slab with two figures.

WESTON BEGGARD *St John The Baptist*   SO 584412

The doorways and chancel arch date the nave to c1200, although it was much rebuilt in 1881. The west tower, south porch, and chancel with two splendid tomb recesses are all of the 14th century.

WESTON-UNDER-PENYARD *St Lawrence*   SO 632232

The nave and four bay north arcade are Late Norman. The aisle was rebuilt in the 14th century, and a porch and west tower then added. The 13th century chancel has three eastern lancets. The nave has an old single framed roof, and there is a 17th century brass memorial.

WHITBOURNE *St John The Baptist*   SO 725570

The nave south doorway with chevrons is Late Norman, and there is a Norman font with interlocked rosettes. The chancel and nave south wall are 13th century, the west tower and two south windows are 14th century, the chancel east wall is 15th century, and the aisle is of 1866. Inside is a tablet to Bellingham Freeman, d1689.

WHITCHURCH *St Dubricius*   SO 557175

The nave and chancel with single framed roofs are 14th century. The south windows are later, the aisle is Victorian, and the font Norman.

WHITNEY *St Peter and St Paul*   SO 267475

The church was mostly rebuilt in 1740 after a flood of the River
Wye, but old masonry can be seen on the north side of the nave and
west tower. The pulpit and reredos incorporate Jacobean material.
The west gallery must be of c1740. The panelling is older, and there
is a door dated 1704, and a tablet to Thomas Williams, d1698.

WIGMORE *St James*   SO 413690

The wide Early Norman nave has herringbone masonry on the northern
side, and an original window, now internal, on the south. The west
tower, chancel, and the south aisle with a two bay arcade and its
original roof with foiled wind braces are 14th century, whilst the
nave roof, with cusped wind braces, and the north chapel, of which
only one bay now remains, are 15th century. The pulpit is early
16th century, and there are traceried old fronts to the stalls.

WILLERSLEY *St Mary Magdalene*   SO 312474

This single chamber church now forms a private house. The Norman
south doorway has rosettes, squares, and chevrons on the lintel. On
the north side are a Norman window and a small 13th century lancet.

WINFORTON *St Michael*   SO 298470

The timber framed upper stage of the pyramidal roofed west tower
is 16th century. The base may go back to the 13th century, the age
of the nave south doorway. Two windows are of c1300, but most have
been renewed. the pulpit is dated 1613, and the communion rail was
given in 1701, whilst the organ case is also early 18th century.

WITHINGTON *St Peter*   SO 566435

The chancel, mostly rebuilt apart from one lancet, forms a single
chamber with a nave with two Late Norman doorways. The west tower
with a recessed spire is 14th century, two south doorways are 15th
century, and the screen with a cornice and cresting is of c1500.

WOLFERLOW *St Andrew*   SO 668618

The church is mostly of 1863 and 1890-4, but the bell turret lies
on old posts, the chancel arch, two doorways, and much of the north
wall are Norman, and there is a late 13th century female effigy.

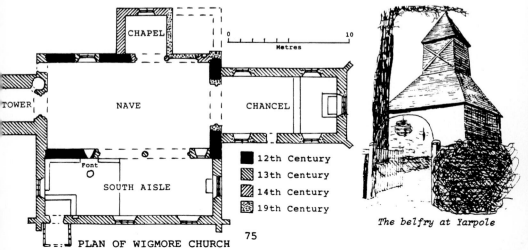

CHAPEL

0 | | | | | 10
Metres

TOWER

NAVE

CHANCEL

Font
O

SOUTH AISLE

■ 12th Century
▨ 13th Century
▧ 14th Century
▩ 19th Century

The belfry at Yarpole

75

PLAN OF WIGMORE CHURCH

WOOLHOPE *St George*   SO 612358

The chancel has one Norman window, perhaps re-set, and there is a
Norman two bay arcade. The aisle was widened and lengthened with a
two bay arcade towards the chancel in c1300. The west tower and the
south aisle were also built in c1300, but the aisle and its arcade
are mostly renewed. In the north aisle are coffin lids of the 13th
and 14th centuries with a lady in profile, and crosses and foliage,
and a 14th century effigy under a canopy with ballflowers.

WORMBRIDGE *St Peter*   SO 427307

The nave has a north doorway of c1200 with several 13th century
lancets, and the west tower is 13th century. The bell stage, parts
of the nave, and all of the chancel, date from the restoration of
1851-9. Under the tower and in the nave are portions of Jacobean
woodwork brought here in 1870 from Newnham Paddox, near Lutterworth.
There are fragments of 15th century glass in the chancel windows.

WORMSLEY *St Mary*   SO 427478

This church is now cared for by the Redundant Churches Fund. It has
a Norman nave with two original windows, a south doorway with an
incised trellis and lozenges, and a 14th century north doorway and
window. The chancel is 13th century, and there is a Jacobean pulpit.

YARKHILL *St John The Baptist*   SO 608427

The church was entirely rebuilt in 1862 except for the 13th century
south doorway, and the west tower, also 13th century, but with a
Norman tower arch, and a top of c1460. There are various old fonts.

YARPOLE *St Leonard*   SO 470648

The nave and chancel were of c1300, but Scott rebuilt the latter in
1864, and added the north aisle. The nave roof with tie-beams and
kingposts is original, and there is a 12th or 13th century font.
The church's claim to architectural fame is the detached tower to
the south, probably of the 14th century, and having an original
door. It is a wooden structure carried on four posts set within a
stone outer wall. On top is a truncated pyramidal roof and spire.

YATTON *All Saints*   SO 627304

The old chapel by Chapel Farm is a humble single chamber, Norman
in origin, with a doorway of that date, but with two 13th century
windows, and rebuilding on the north and east sides in the 16th or
17th centuries and 1704 respectively. It is now disused. Probably
from it are the posts and top rail of the screen in the new church
of 1841 by William Roberts, which also has two 16th century foreign
reliefs of Christ before Pilate and The Resurrection, and a lectern
with late 17th century work.

YAZOR *St John The Baptist*   SO 404464

The ruins of the old church lie to the south of the new church of
1843 by George Rowe, to which the Price family monuments have been
transferred. The remains comprise a 15th century three bay arcade
joining a 13th or 14th century west tower to a south transept of
c1300 which occupied most of the south side, leaving space for an
aisle only one bay long to the west.